You Have to Scream
with Your Mouth Shut

Violence in the Home

Karina Colgan

ACKNOWEDGEMENTS

I would like to convey my sincere thanks to the many people who without hesitation gave their time to contribute in some way to this book. I am deeply indebted to all the women, men and children who spoke so openly and honestly to me. Their courage and dignity inspired me. Their names have been changed to protect their identities.

The following peole went above and beyond the call of duty to assist me with my research: John Lonergan, Governor, Mountjoy Prison, Dr Art O'Connor, Consultant Forensic Psychiatrist, Central Mental Hospital, Roisin McDermott, Director, Women's Aid, Phil Power, Director, Aoibhneas Women's Refuge, Tammy Berry, Social Care Worker, Pat Finnett, MOVE Ireland, Kathleen McMahon, Chief Officer, and Martin Butler, Mountjoy Women's Prison. I would also like to thank the following: Vincent McPherson, Governor, Wheatfield Prison, John Moore, *News of the World*, Ken Divine, Stena Sealink, Barry O'Sullivan, Pembroke, Ivan Barratt, Jane McDonnell, Editor, *Image* Magazine, Joe Broderick, Anna Farmar and all those who wish to remain anonymous. My thanks to you all.

Those closest to me deserve a special mention, because they are the ones who made it all possible: my mother and mentor, Christina Berry, for all her literary and motherly advice, not to mention her love, support, encouragement, guidance and unlimited babysitting; my beloved children, Karl and Sarah, who once again showed enormous patience and actually allowed mummy to work in peace occasionally; Tanya-Samantha; Mary O'Sullivan to whom I will always be grateful, for her constant and continuing help and support; my publishers, who shared my conviction that this was a book worth publishing. Finally, the biggest thanks have to go to my husband and best friend, Gerry, without whose love and support this book would not have been possible. He is a man I am very lucky to have married.

This book is dedicated to the memory of my father, Trevor, who died suddenly on 21 June 1994, and who had looked forward to seeing it in print.

'With Christ which is far better'
(Phillipians 1: 23)

CONTENTS

ALL NAMES HAVE BEEN CHANGED TO
PROTECT IDENTITIES

Introduction

'When we reached our house he dragged me out of the car by my hair. He said that if I made a sound he would kill me and the baby. He opened the front door and pushed me in so hard that I fell. I pleaded with him not to hurt the baby, I didn't care about myself. He reminded me that I had an appointment with the doctor the following day and told me that it wouldn't be the thing to beat me now. Instead, he told me that he was going to punish me. He dragged me into the kitchen and made me sit with my hands outstretched on the table. He went to the cupboard, took out the hammer and came back to the table. He said that if I moved or made a sound he would smash my skull, then he calmly asked me which two fingers I wanted broken. I really thought that he was just trying to frighten me, trying to teach me a lesson. Soon I realised that he wasn't – he said that I had ten seconds to decide and that if I didn't tell him, he was going to break every one of my fingers.

'When I realised that he wasn't bluffing, I tried to reason with him. I told him that the doctor would want to know how I had managed to break two fingers. He just laughed and said that I would have all night to think of a plausible excuse. Then, without any warning, he lifted the hammer and smashed it down on to the last two fingers of my left hand. For a moment I was too shocked to feel anything but then the pain began. When I screamed in agony, he told me to shut my mouth unless I wanted him to do the same thing to my other hand. I remember sitting there thinking that I was going to pass out from the pain. He made me sit on the chair all night without moving, I had to urinate without moving off the chair. I felt so humiliated.

I prayed that he would fall asleep so I could tend to my fingers and change my clothes that were soaked with urine. Finally, after ten hours, he told me to go and clean myself up before I went to the doctor. My fingers were swollen and bruised and I couldn't manger to undress myself. When he saw the difficulty I was having, he got a scissors and cut my clothes off me. I closed my eyes, and in a way I hoped that he would kill me.'

Sandra is one of the many women and men who shared their stories with me, in order that that the appalling crime of violence in the home against women and children (and occasionally men) be highlighted. They want to let people who live in fear know that is there is help available and that there are people who care. Help is often only a phone call away.

Before writing this book, I, like many others, was not aware of the extent of violence in the home directed at women and children. This was an issue that did not concern me personally and I gave it thought only when the media focused on individual cases. Then one day I began to question what happens to all those victims who are not the subject of media attention and whose situations are not resolved.

When I began my research for this book I was not prepared for the horrific tales of abuse, the frightening worldwide statistics in relation to this crime, the apparent lack of interest of the Irish law and the appalling lack of support for the victim. As I continued, it became evident to me that this crime, though it is of epidemic proportions, is very often not reported. Globally, for every one crime of violence in the home that *is* reported, there will be at least another five that are not. Shocking statistics do little to give rise to action on the part of governments and domestic violence is still not recognised as an urgent 'social issue'. The crime of violence in the home can leave victims scarred, maimed, battered, disabled, disfigured or even fatally injured, often without anyone knowing that it is going on until it is too late. My research shows that a woman will on average sustain fifteen bad beatings before going to a refuge. These refuges and safe houses are themselves inadequately funded and all rely on donations and fundraising to maintain even the most basic service – a service I feel should be readily available to those who are in need of it.

Domestic violence conjures up an image of a woman being battered by her husband. Although this scenario would be true of the majority of cases of violence in the home, it is not the only type of violence, and women are not always the only victims. This crime is often stereotyped, particularly as regards social class. This type of violence crosses all social, cultural, economic and political divides. It is not more prevalent in any class. It does not consist only of physical violence but may also involve other types of violence – horrific mental and sexual abuse. Very often a woman will be subjected to all three. Many will never fully recover from its effects.

Refuges and helplines are inundated with calls from

victims wanting to escape, but not always having the courage or resources to do so. For refuges the busiest time of the year is Christmas. I find it incredible that in the city of Dublin, there is a total of sixteen refuge spaces available for a population of one million people. I question why a woman must wait up to ten months for an appointment with a solicitor for Free Legal Aid. Women who are not married and living with a partner are not afforded the same rights as a married woman. Ireland is one of the few countries that has no official statistics documenting the extent of this problem.

The people whose stories I tell in this book have all been involved in a violent situation in the home. Most have been abused, a few have abused. All have told me their story in the hope that they will lead to a greater understanding of the phrase 'domestic violence'. A book will not stop the horrific crimes of domestic violence and the silent suffering of all those who are abused in the family home. My intention is to highlight these crimes and perhaps help to make people aware that a very real and frightening problem exists in our society; the voices of the victims must be heard.

I am indebted to all those who spoke so openly and honestly to me, giving me the opportunity to gain an insight into a world I knew little of. All names have been changed to protect identities.

Karina Colgan
September 1994

1

SUE'S STORY

Sue is in her early thirties and has one daughter under ten. Sue and her daughter both suffered at the hands of her abusive husband, and it was only when Sue realised how traumatised her daughter was that she made the decision to leave the family home. It is three years since she left and she has no regrets about her decision. This is her story.

'Goodness, I don't know where to begin. I suppose I never thought of myself as a victim – Mike [her husband] always had a temper but over the years I'd learnt how to deal with this. I suppose I blocked it out, I justified his behaviour by saying that he wasn't the only man in the world who had a temper. Since I left, I must have asked myself a million times why I did not leave sooner. For years I didn't even think about leaving him. You see he was always sorry. If he smashed up the place or hit me, he would be sorry the next day and swear that it would never happen again, I always hoped that he meant it, but he never did and it just went on and on. Before Emma was born, I only had myself to worry about. I could cope with his violence. After Emma was born, I realised that it wasn't fair to her, to bring her up living in fear of her father.

'Mike had a very short fuse and it didn't take much to push him over the edge. Everyone in the family knew about his temper – he'd lost his temper many times when he lived at home He was a bit like the girl in the nursery rhyme – when he was good he was very, very good and when he was bad he was horrid. I threatened to leave him about ten times between the time we were married and when Emma was born. I never actually left though; I just said I would to try and make him see sense. One time he came home in a really foul humour – I knew the minute he came in that something or someone had annoyed him. He was ranting and raving like a lunatic and I knew what was coming next. I tried to get him out of bad humour by suggesting we go out. This was probably the worst thing I could have done. I should have just left the house and gone for a walk. Anyway, with that he came over to me and told me that I didn't care about what had happened to him and all I wanted to do was to go out and enjoy myself. He took his dinner out of the microwave and threw it at me. He threw it so hard, the plate broke when it hit me. I was reeling from the impact and I knew that if I moved he would get even more annoyed, so I stayed still. When I didn't move he started screaming at me was I just going to leave the mess on the floor or what? I made an attempt to clean it up but didn't get very far before he got the swing bin and emptied it on top of me. Then as quickly at it started, it was over. He got down on the floor beside me and said that he was so sorry. He told me to go up and have a bath and he would clear the mess up.

'Another time we were going to a wedding and the car broke down. I could see that he was getting more annoyed by the minute so I didn't open my mouth. He got out of the car and looked under the bonnet and he called for me to go and hold something for him – which I did. He thought that he had fixed what was wrong and when he discovered he hadn't he slammed the bonnet down while I was still holding the wire. I thought I was going to black out with the pain, I remember screaming. He said to me that if it weren't for me none of this would have happened – it was my friend's wedding we were going to. Mike managed to stop a passing motorist and he gave us a jump-start. I spent that afternoon in hospital – he'd broken my wrist. On the way to the hospital I told him that I had had enough and I couldn't take any more. He was pleading with me to forgive him and telling me that he'd change. I was determined that this time I would stick to my guns and go. While I was in having the plaster put on to my wrist, I was thinking about where I would go and about finally telling my parents what was happening. When I came out after having the cast put on, he was waiting for me with six bunches of flowers and a big balloon that said 'I Love You'. He had bought them in the hospital shop. I weakened and we went home and talked. I didn't leave him.

'Since I left him, people have asked me why did I put up with it for so long. The answer is simple: I loved him, and deep down I suppose I didn't really want to leave him. I convinced myself that he would change and every time it happened, I'd say "This will be the last time." I believe that he was sorry that he had done it, but it the end, sorry wasn't enough.

'He was delighted when I announced I was pregnant – he'd always wanted children. He came to all the ante-natal classes with me and was present at the birth. During my pregnancy, once my stomach got big, he treated me as if I was made of china. He kept saying that his baby would bring us closer together and that we'd be a real family now. He was so proud when Emma was born and in the beginning I really thought that Emma would stop his violent behaviour. For a while she did.

'Emma was six months old when she first experienced his violence. She was teething and I had been up most of the night with her. She was screaming with pain and I was doing my best to soothe her, I felt so sorry for her. I had taken her downstairs so that Mike could sleep – he had to be up early for an important meeting. I couldn't stop Emma screaming and Mike came down. As soon as he came into the room I saw the look on his face that I had come to know meant trouble. He was livid and demanded that I keep her quiet because he couldn't sleep with the noise she was making. I told him that she was in pain and he said that he was in pain too with the headache she had given him. He came over to me and grabbed her out of my arms. He shook her really hard and then he threw her on to the couch. As soon as he had done it he was sorry and he stayed up the rest of the night cradling her in his arms.

'It was as if the incident with Emma had broken the spell. Soon he was back to his old ways. I could see that Emma was being affected by the violence and the shouting.

Even as a toddler, she'd run to me when he came in. Once she spilt something on his papers and he went mad. He picked her up and threw her across the room. I ran in when I heard her screaming and Mike was picking her up off the floor. I asked what had happened and he said that he had pushed her. As he spoke, I could see a bump forming on her forehead. Emma was hysterical and wouldn't go to Mike – she kept saying "Bold daddy, bold daddy." Mike kept saying to me that he hadn't meant to push her away as hard as he did. Emma stopped crying and Mike suggested we all go to McDonald's to cheer her up. By that evening, Emma was pals with Mike again and I tried to reason things out. If I'm honest, I made excuses for him.

'Emma was about three-and-a-half when she started saying "Daddy no nice, daddy go away." It was around this time that Mike seemed to be in bad humour all the time. I knew that he was under a lot of pressure in work but he was constantly lashing out at me and Emma. If he was punching me, Emma would try to pull him away. More often than not she'd get a blow too. When I'd bring her up to bed after there had been an argument, she would say to me "Mummy, make daddy go away." My mind was twisted and I felt that I was being torn in two. I knew that things couldn't go on like they were and I decided to try and talk to Mike.

'I explained to him that he was hurting Emma and that I couldn't allow it to continue. He said that Emma knew that he didn't mean to do it and that he never meant to hit her. I asked him did he not realise what he was doing and he replied that all children get a smack now and then.

He didn't seem to realise how wrong what he was doing was. He actually came to me one night and asked me why Emma seemed to be afraid of him?

'What made it so difficult for me to make the decision to leave was that when Mike wasn't violent, he was a loving husband and father. He would come in with presents for me and Emma for no reason. We often went out as a family and had some very good times. He could be so loving and tender and I knew that he did love me and Emma. Towards the end I realised that he was never going to change and that if I stayed my daughter was going to be severely affected for the rest of her life. She was showing signs of being affected before I left. She began wetting the bed and told me many times that she didn't want to leave me alone with daddy in case he hit me. She often asked me why her daddy hit us and why we were bold. She would frequently say to me: "I'm a good girl, aren't I?"

'The last straw was during another of Mike's violent attacks, when he threw a vase at me, but it missed me and hit Emma. She was hysterical and told me that she wanted to go to her granny. She couldn't go to school the next day because she had a black eye. When Mike went to work that day I knew that it was now or never. The sight of my five-year-old daughter with a black eye finally brought home the fact that things would never be any different. As it was, I knew that Mike had got worse. So many things went through my head as I made the decision to leave. I thought of our wedding day, I thought of the day Emma was born, I thought of all the happy times we'd had ... but then I thought of all the times I'd been punched, all the times I couldn't move outside the door because people would see the bruises. I thought of all the times I'd avoided my neighbour out of embarrassment because I knew that she'd heard the fight. I thought of the times I'd had to go to Casualty with injuries he'd given me, I thought of all the times he'd said sorry and how over the years sorry had become just another word. I thought of how I had lived in terror and realised that I had always watched what I said and did in case it annoyed Mike. I realised that I could not win with Mike – that his temper was part of him and that I couldn't change that.

'What I thought about most, though, was Emma. I thought about all the times she had screamed in fear and the times she had pleaded with Mike not to hit her. I saw her little face contorted with terror when Mike hit me. I saw her crumpled like a little rag doll after Mike had hit her. I saw the way she would look at Mike when she knew he wasn't watching and I thought about the time I had overheard her saying her prayers and asking God to make daddy go away so she and mummy wouldn't be frightened any more. I knew that I had to take Emma and leave.

'Once I had made the decision, I found it surprisingly easy to act. I had the difficult task of ringing my mother and asking if we could stay with her. She was super and said that I should have confided in her all along. She came over and helped me to pack. Emma was delighted that we were leaving and when she knew that I had told my mother about what had been happening she told her granny about how bold her daddy was. I saw a solicitor that afternoon about a separation and, as expected, Mike came around to my mother's that evening. My father spoke to him and told him that when I was ready I would contact him. Mike didn't put up a fight. In a way I think he knew this was coming.

'My solicitor was great and I pretty much left things to her. I wasn't out to get Mike and I wanted to be as fair as possible. All things considered, it was a very amicable parting. When I saw Mike a couple of weeks after I left, I told him that I loved him but I could no longer live with him. I explained that it would take me a long time to forgive him for what he had put me and Emma through and that I would never forget what he had done. I think that he accepted that it was over and as a gesture of goodwill, he applied for an overseas transfer. He was successful and almost a year after I left, he moved to America. He signed the house over to me and sends money to me.

'Emma and I moved back home a year after we left and started a brand new life. Emma is a different child now that she no longer lives in fear. She is a happy and outgoing child and no longer wets the bed. I told her that daddy was sick and didn't mean to do what he did. She accepted this explanation and thrived once she knew that Mike wouldn't be living with us any more.

'Mike has kept in touch and Emma writes to him regularly – it's as if she knows that he is far away and can't come home. Now she says "I love my daddy but I don't want him to come home." Mike has been back a few times since he went away and we all went out for a meal. Emma goes out with him when he is home and they have a good time together. Mike doesn't come to the house, though, in case it upsets Emma. In time, I hope the memories will fade. Recently I have gone back to work and for the first time in many years, I feel that I am my own person. Little things mean so much: it's great to decide on the spur of the moment to go out with Emma and have pizza for tea. I don't have room in my life now for another man – Emma is my world and I feel that I have so much to do to make it up to her.'

2

SANDRA'S STORY

Sandra is thirty-four years old, married and lives in the west of Ireland. She has three children under the age of ten. She has been a victim of domestic violence for the past ten years and had a miscarriage as a result of a severe beating. She is still living with her husband and is still being beaten by him. She feels that there is no way out at the moment and dreams of the day when her children are grown and she can finally escape. She told me that she made the decision to stay in this situation for the sake of her children, who know nothing about the beatings. Sandra is not alone; there are thousands of women in similar situations. This is Sandra's story.

'The first time I met my husband, Robert, was at a friend's wedding. I had just broken up with my boyfriend and I was feeling pretty vulnerable. When I was introduced to Robert I couldn't help noticing how handsome he was. The fact he was far older than me didn't bother me at all. We talked to each other for the rest of the night, and when he asked if I would meet him again I jumped at the chance.

'We met the following week and after he left me home I pinched myself to see whether or not I was dreaming. I pinched myself quite a lot in those early years and when on the third anniversary of our first date he asked me to marry him, I said yes. I had no reason to say no: for three years he had been the perfect gentleman. He always opened doors for me, always respected that I wanted to remain a virgin until I married. We didn't argue much and he seemed to spend all his time trying to make me happy. He didn't have to, though, I *was* happy. I can honestly say that there was no indication of his bad temper or of his other side in the years before we married.

'In time, my family and friends knew that the relationship was serious and began to accept Robert. He was more than ten years older than me and it took people a while to realise that this didn't matter to us. All that mattered was that we were happy and in love. When I announced we were getting married, my parents said that if I was happy then they were happy too and gave their blessing. Plans were made for the wedding and before I knew it, I was walking down the aisle. As I said "I do", I looked into Robert's eyes and hoped that he was as happy as I was.

'We had the reception at a local hotel and at 10.30 pm we left for the airport. We went to Greece for our honeymoon. The first week of our holiday was perfect but the second week the troubled started. We had spent the day walking and when we got back to the hotel, I wanted to lie down for an hour. I was exhausted and just wanted to sleep, Robert however, wanted to go dancing. When I asked him to wait until I had rested he got very annoyed and began shouting at me. He was like a different man – it was a side of him that I had never seen before. I gave in to his demands and went dancing. As the night wore on, and after drinking heavily, he got more aggressive. It seemed that anything I said or did made him worse, I couldn't win. He started accusing me of flirting with the waiters and said that I was his and I was never to look at another man again. I couldn't understand what was happening and later that night, when we got back to our room I received my first beating. When he was finished hitting me, he said that what he had just done was only a taste of what he would do if he ever saw me looking at another man again. Then he calmly went to bed.

'I was afraid to get up off the floor for a long time. I tried to put the corner of my blouse up my nose to stop it bleeding. When I did get up and saw my face in the mirror, I couldn't think straight. I tried to reason why he had done this. I felt that it was my fault. Although I hadn't flirted with the waiter, perhaps I shouldn't have smiled when I thanked him for the wine. I went to bed that night not knowing what would happen next. The next thing I knew Robert was shaking me. He told me to go in to the bathroom and put some make-up on – he wanted to go down for breakfast. I did as he asked. He acted as if nothing had happened and when I asked him for an explanation he just said that I deserved what I got. He said that it was over and done with and to forget about it. He was back to his old self and suggested that we spend the day sailing. During the day, he told me that he was sorry for hitting me, but it had to be done. I was so mixed up and confused that he managed to convince me that, I had been responsible for it happening and I ended up apologising to him. Although I was very upset about this, I accepted what he said and made a mental note to try harder. I wanted this marriage to work, I loved Robert. The rest of our holiday was without incident and we returned home.

'It was eight months before he beat me again. This time I knew that he was angry and I tried to talk to him on the way home. We had been at a family gathering and I had spent most of the evening talking to a friend of my brother's; we were talking about how to throw a surprise engagement party for his girlfriend. I saw Robert making his way towards us with a very annoyed expression. When he reached me he grabbed my arm and told me that we were leaving. I had no time to say goodbye to anybody, I didn't even have time to get my coat. When we got into the car, my head smacked off the door as he pushed me in. I was frightened and tried to think of a way I could make him understand that I hadn't meant to upset him. My efforts were futile. The only thing he said on the way home was: "I told you what would happen if you flirted with a man." I thought about trying to jump out of the car but I decided not to because it was freezing cold. I had no coat, no money, it was miles from anywhere and I was six months pregnant. I tried to reassure myself that he wouldn't hit me when I was so heavily pregnant. I was wrong.

'When we reached our house he dragged me out of the car by my hair. He said that if I made a sound he would kill me and the baby. He opened the door and pushed me in so hard that I fell. I pleaded with him not to hurt the baby. I didn't care about myself. He reminded me that I had an appointment with the doctor the following day and said that it wouldn't be the thing to beat me now. Instead he said he'd punish me. He dragged me into the kitchen and made me sit with my hands outstretched on the table. He went to the press, took out the hammer and came back to the table. He said that if I moved he would smash my skull. Then he asked me which two fingers I wanted broken. I really thought he was just trying to frighten me to teach me a lesson. Soon I realised that he wasn't. He said that I had ten seconds to tell him. If I didn't he was going to break all of my fingers.

'When I realised that he wasn't bluffing, I tried to reason with him. I told him that the doctor would want to know how I managed to break two fingers. He just laughed and said that I would have all night to think of a plausible excuse. Then without any warning he lifted the hammer and smashed it down on to the last two fingers of my left hand.

'For a moment I was too shocked to feel anything but then the pain started. When I screamed in agony he told me to shut my mouth unless I wanted the same done to my right hand. I remember sitting there thinking I was going to pass out from the pain. He made me sit at that table all night without moving, I had to urinate sitting on the chair; I felt so humiliated. I prayed that he would fall asleep so that I could tend to my fingers. Finally, after ten hours, he told me to clean myself up before I went to the doctor. My fingers were so swollen and bruised, I couldn't take off my clothes. When he saw the difficulty I was having getting undressed, he got a scissors and cut my clothes off. I shut my eyes, and in a way I hoped that he would kill me.

'The doctor was horrified when he saw my fingers and asked me why I had left it so long. I didn't know what to say to him, I almost told him the truth but then I thought about what would happen to me if I did. Instead I just said that it was too late to call him out especially when I was seeing him the next morning. I must have looked like a wreck because he asked me how things were at home and if everything was all right. I replied that everything was fine.

'When I got home from the doctor, Robert was fast asleep in bed. I crept into the other bedroom and lay on the bed, I was so tired. The next thing I knew Robert was shaking me, telling me he was hungry. It was quite hard to make dinner with two broken fingers.

'The night our daughter was born, Robert accused me of smiling at the doctor that delivered the baby. I was too tired to argue but still tried to explain that the only reason I had smiled was because the doctor had said congratulations. Robert seemed to accept this, probably because he didn't want to make a scene in front of so many people. He still punished me though; that afternoon I had no visitors. Robert had told my family and his that I had said I wanted no visitors. He said to them that I was suffering from depression. When visitors came in the next day they were very subdued. Once again, Robert had ruined what should have been a very happy time for us.

'Our daughter was fifteen weeks old when he beat me again. I had been up most of the night with her trying to keep her quiet so that she wouldn't wake Robert. I dozed off about 6.30 am on a chair in the sitting room. At 7.30

I was pulled off the chair by my hair. Robert was screaming at me because I didn't have his breakfast ready. He dragged me into the kitchen and flung me at the table, then he went to the fridge and took out eggs and sausages. He threw the eggs at me one by one and then wrapped the sausages around my neck. He said that he was going to pour petrol all over me and set it alight – that way he said he could be sure that I was cooking his breakfast. The baby started crying and thankfully he just stormed out to work.

'The beatings were more frequent from then on and after the birth of our second child. I felt that I was really trapped. I could see no way out and I had nobody to talk to. I couldn't tell a single person about my living hell. It got to the stage where I had to go to neighbouring towns to attend casualty departments. The casualty department in my local hospital was beginning to get suspicious. I didn't want to arouse suspicion in case my children were taken away from me. I tried to patch myself up for a while.

'I was nine weeks pregnant with our third child when, after a long drinking session with some of his friends, Robert came home and beat me so badly I lost our baby. It took me a long time to recover from this. I had accepted five long years of beatings, torture and cruelty. I could not accept that he had killed our baby. He said to me that it wasn't a baby anyway. It was from this point that I began to lose faith in myself and my beliefs. I began to think that somehow, all of this was my own doing. I resigned myself to the fact that this was how life was going to be and I would have to learn to live with it. I had no choice; it was either this or I would have to kill him. I knew that

I couldn't kill him. I couldn't even bring myself to kill a fly. I dreamed about what life would be like without him and I did pray that he would drop dead of a heart attack. But this didn't happen and the beatings continued.

'When I became pregnant again, it was nine months of hell. I was determined that nothing would happen to this baby. I had to spend twenty-four hours a day protecting the baby. I was afraid to sleep in case he would come in drunk and hit me. I would wait until he was asleep before I went to sleep myself. I used to sleep with one leg out of the bed because I felt that in this way I would have a better chance of escaping from him, if he woke up in a bad humour.

'Towards the end of the pregnancy, I was taken into hospital because my blood pressure was very high. I was in hospital for three weeks before the birth and I was able to relax. I knew that here I was safe, and more importantly now the baby would be safe too. For the first time in a long while, I was able to sleep at night without the fear of being beaten. I began to eat properly and even began to feel like a normal person. Robert didn't come to visit very often. A neighbour brought the children to see me every other day and Robert would bring them to see me on Sunday. I missed the children and they missed me but, they were happy to be staying with the neighbour. It was like a holiday for them. When I gave birth to a baby boy, I cried bitter tears. People thought I was crying with happiness, but I was crying because now, I would have to return home to my living hell.

'Within two weeks the beatings started again. I had to postpone my six-week check-up at the hospital because I was covered in bruises. I now lived only for the children. I thought about ending my life many times. The only thing that stopped me was my trust in God. Robert never hurt the children. He was a fairly good father when he was in a good mood. He didn't lash out at the children the way he lashed out at me.

'I remember one incident in particular – I will never forget it. It was our eighth wedding anniversary. We never celebrated any wedding anniversary; Robert said that there was nothing to celebrate and he was right. However, this particular year, before he left for work, he told me to organise a babysitter for that night as we were going out for a meal. Before I had a chance to say anything, he was gone.

'I spent the day wondering if things were going to change. Even at this stage I prayed that things might get better. I was more than prepared to make a fresh start, although Robert had made my life an absolute hell for eight years, I still wanted the man I had married back, I thought I still loved him.

'Robert telephoned to say that he had to work late and arranged to meet me at a restaurant. There was nothing in his tone to indicate anything was different; he was terse and to the point. I got the children to bed early and spent ages getting myself ready. I wanted to try and look as good as I possibly could. I spent a long time putting my make-up on and deciding what to wear. When I was ready and looked at myself in the mirror, I actually felt good. All the time I had spent getting ready was worth it.

'On the taxi journey to the restaurant, I dreamed about the night that lay ahead. Maybe Robert had finally realised what he was doing, maybe he was going to suggest that we start again. My mind was racing. There hadn't been a beating now for over a month. It was tough going, but I wasn't giving Robert any opportunity to fault me.

'I arrived at the restaurant at 9.03 pm. Robert wasn't outside, so I decided to wait for him. At 9.30 pm, there was still no sign of him so I decided to go into the restaurant to see whether or not he had telephoned to say that he would be late. As I went inside, I saw Robert sitting at a table. I was shocked to see him there. I went over to him and said that I had been waiting outside for the previous half hour. He told me that it was time to leave. He said that he told me to be there at 9.00 pm and I was late. I tried to explain that I was there at 9.03 pm but he wasn't interested. With a sinking feeling, I realised that nothing had changed or ever would change. I didn't say a word on the way home; there was no point.

'When we got home, he paid the babysitter and she went home. I asked him why had he arranged to go out at all and he said that he just wanted to prove that I was still flirting with other men. He told me that I looked like a tart and asked me did I make an arrangement to meet the taxi driver again. I said to him that I hadn't even spoken to the taxi driver because I was too busy looking forward to the night out. There was no reasoning with him and as his fist connected with my face, I knew that there was never going to be a fresh start.

'I have taken ten years of this abuse and the only thing I dream about now is that my children will be grown up and I can leave him. I am sure people who read my story will ask why I don't leave him now but it's not as easy as that. It wouldn't be fair to uproot the children and take them away from their home and friends. They don't know what is going on and that's the way I'll keep it. I've learnt to scream with my mouth shut and at least Robert never hits me in front of the children. I know that if I did leave Robert would find me and then things would be even worse. I have accepted that this is how my life is going to be, I have to try and make the best of it for the sake of my children. If I had no children I would be gone long ago. The love I had for Robert is gone. The thing I find hardest to cope with is the fact that everybody thinks that Robert is such a nice man. People see a devoted father and loving husband, a man who provides for his family and has a good job. Nobody sees the man who lives at home with me.'

3

MEGAN'S STORY

Megan is thirty-six years old, married, and has five children ranging in age from six to seventeen. When I spoke to her, she had been living at the refuge for two weeks. She is currently fighting for custody of her three youngest children. She doesn't want the house, just her children. 'I will start off in a hovel once I have the children. If it's a case that I don't get the children then I won't be around any longer.' Megan has left behind all the trappings of a comfortable middle-class lifestyle. Her only concern now, after fleeing from an abusive relationship, is to get custody of her children and start to rebuild a new life. 'If I don't get my children, by the time this book comes out I'll be dead.'

'I first met Paddy when I was thirteen years old and he was thirty-seven. After my father died we were put into children's homes. Paddy was a 'house father' to my brothers. When I went to visit my brothers I would see Paddy and we would have a chat. He was a father figure to me and a very nice guy. When my brothers left his care, he said to me to continue visiting him to have a chat. A relationship developed and we married when I was seventeen. We were three months married when I got pregnant. The landlord of the flat we were living in said that he wouldn't allow children so I went back to live with my mother and Paddy stayed in the flat. Paddy wouldn't come to live in my mother's house because he hated her. So did I but I had no choice. My mother was an alcoholic. When the baby was born, Paddy wouldn't come to the christening because the party was at my mother's house.

'When the baby was six months old we got a flat on the north side of the city. By now there was no relationship to speak of between us and I realised I had married him for all the wrong reasons. For a while everything was fine and we had another baby a year and ten months later. I had wanted a father figure when I got married, but as I got older I wanted more than that. We never really had a marriage. In the eighteen years that we have been married I'd say that we have made love no more than thirty times. As time went on I wanted more than friendship. Eventually I became a compulsive gambler. I used to say to Paddy that I wanted to make love and he would reply that he couldn't because he couldn't trust me. I believed him and for eighteen years I was full of guilt about it.

'We lived in this flat for eight years. During this time I left him once. I was still gambling and I suppose in a way I ran away from my responsibilities and from the horrible feeling of being unloved. I stayed with my mother for three months and used to visit the kids regularly. Paddy was very nice about it. He got a home help for the kids because he couldn't manage with the four of them.

In the end I went back because I missed the kids too much and I was afraid that they would be taken into care. Soon after I returned, we moved to a new house. Things got a bit better and most of our time was spent doing up the house. There was very little physical contact between myself and Paddy and I began to gamble again.

'After we were in the new house about a year, I decided that I had enough. I had no self-esteem and felt that I was nothing. I decided to go for treatment and was eight weeks in treatment. I realised for the first time that I was worth something and that I wasn't a bad person. It was only then I realised how hurt I really was and how gambling had become my friend. One day they asked me about Paddy and I wouldn't answer. They asked me what I was afraid of and I replied that Paddy had told me that I was an unfit mother and that I would never get custody of my kids. I went for treatment to prove that I could conquer the compulsive gambling and because my kids were the most important things in my life.

'It was only after I went for treatment that the trouble really started. Paddy couldn't blame me any longer for his lack of sex drive. Now everything was fine for me and the children just as I had always wanted. I was glad I wasn't lost any longer. He had lost his crutch, though. When I stopped gambling and started taking care of the kids and the house, he couldn't run to my family and say she's done this, that or the other. He couldn't get sympathy any longer. The mental abuse started then because I was "coping". He couldn't say "poor you" any longer and he resented me for that. The mental abuse started in relation to sex. If I wanted to make love he would tell me that I was only there to look after the kids and cook dinner. He became very aggressive even with the kids. He used to work nights and when the kids came in from school they would have to whisper. They were not allowed to play and if someone woke him up there would be awful trouble.

'Finally, after ten years, I began to answer him back. I was supposed to be grateful that he was there. He had a good job and gave me money every week but if I ran short during the week and asked him for a loan of five pounds, he would get me to list everything I had spent my money on. It got to the stage that I had to keep receipts for everything so he could see what I was spending the money on. When I came out after having treatment, I made new friends and for the first time ever I had somebody other than him to rely on. He didn't like the fact that I had friends and that I wasn't gambling. I'd go to the weekly meetings and he'd say to me "Why are you going to those – sure you don't gamble." He didn't want me going out and made me feel very guilty when I went. Although I knew that I needed the meetings, in the end, I did stop going because of him. It just wasn't worth the hassle every time I went. When I stopped going, everything was fine, I got the impression that he always hoped I would start gambling again. I kept my head straight for seven years and just got on with things. I didn't gamble.

'From the time our son (who is now six years old) was conceived we slept in separate rooms. When he was two I got a job. This completely freaked Paddy out; now I wasn't financially dependent on him. I think this is what finally did it – I didn't have to ask him for money any more. It was a full-time job. I bought a small car and that was *mine*.

It was the only thing I could say was mine and it was my pride and joy. A couple of months later I was on my way home from the shops when I had a major car crash. A drunk ran into the car from behind I was thrown through the windscreen. The car was a write-off and I was very badly injured. I had two broken legs and other injuries and my face was a complete mess. I was in hospital for ten weeks. When I saw my face for the first time after the crash I wanted to get plastic surgery. When I came home from the hospital the kids were afraid of me. Paddy kept telling me not go get plastic surgery; he said that he didn't mind. For six months I didn't move outside the door, again I was dependent on him. Looking back, I know now that he didn't want me to get plastic surgery because if my face was fixed up then I would go out again.

'Five months after the crash I had plastic surgery on my face. Two months later I had more. I didn't move outside the house during this time and things couldn't have been better at home. However, after my second operation, I wanted to return to work. I felt that I was ready and I knew that returning to work would help me to feel 'normal' again. I now began to work from 5.00 am– 2.30 pm five days a week. This worked out well because it meant that I was at home with the children during the day. Paddy never did anything in the house; he used to tell me to tell the kids to do it. I had been made to clean the house from when I was five years old and I wasn't going to let the same thing happen to my children. Paddy couldn't understand this. I would come home at 2.30 pm and start cleaning the house. He complained that I wasn't spending enough time with him; he said that I was never there. This wasn't true – it was just because he didn't like me working. We knew that things were coming to a head. We weren't getting on and it was becoming more difficult to even be civil to each other. One day I asked him to leave, I told him that I wanted a separation. A huge fight followed and then he told me that he would leave. He called all the kids into the sitting room and told them that he was leaving and that he wouldn't be able to see them ever again. He told them that he wouldn't be able to afford to take them out and that he wouldn't even be able to afford to buy a kettle or a bed. He said that he would have to sleep on the floor of his flat. The three youngest were hysterical, I could see the game he was playing. The two youngest came over to me and started to give out to me because I was throwing daddy out. They begged me to let him stay, so rather than put them through any more, I gave in and he stayed. We never made up, it was just taken for granted that he would be staying.

'At this stage he was becoming more aggressive. He kept telling me that he wanted me out of the house. He said that if anyone left it would be me. I wouldn't give in to him, I wasn't leaving my kids or my home for anybody. I put up with it rather than leave. It got to the stage where we wouldn't talk to each other for weeks on end. He would run me down all the time in front of the children and instead of talking to me himself, he would say to one of the kids: "Tell your mother." It was around this time that I did a personal development course. I wasn't feeling good about myself at all and didn't know how much more I could take. I asked Paddy to come for counselling with me and he agreed. The row we had in front of the counsellor was unbelievable. He told her that it was all my fault and that he couldn't love me. The counsellor was the person who suggested that I do the course. It lasted six weeks and when I finished it I did feel better. Paddy said that he didn't like my attitude; it was all wrong as far as he was concerned. When I said that I wanted more than a platonic relationship, he replied that we should sit down and talk. We decided that we would stay together for the sake of the kids but we would "live our own lives". I said that was fine by me and then he dropped the bombshell. He said that if I met someone else that was fine with him as long as I didn't tell him about it. This hurt me more than anyone will ever know, I felt lower than a doormat at this moment to think that he didn't want me.

'Soon after this decision I was awarded compensation for the car crash. It was a fairly big amount, £36,000. As we had decided to stay together for the sake of the children, I put £22,000 into the house. It was like a little mansion and I loved it. I bought myself a car and I even bought Paddy a motor bike. I spent all the money on the family and it was soon gone and then I went back to work. At least now my wages were my own, I had no bills hanging over me. I saved for weeks to buy my son a computer which cost £800 and Paddy went mad over this. He said that I did not consult him and that he felt that he wasn't being included. Again my self-esteem began to go. My wages went on things for the house. When I brought something home he would say to me "You never asked me if you could get that." I didn't gamble one penny of the money but the elation I felt over this was quickly wiped out by the way Paddy was going on.

'The doctors told me that I had cervical cancer and had to have laser treatment. I would have further checks after six months, twelve months, eighteen months and twenty-four months and then get a clean bill of health.

'The kitchen sink got blocked and it was stuck for a few days. To empty the sink you had to get under the sink, unscrew the pipe and let the water out into a basin. I came in from work one night and Paddy had the whole kitchen flooded from trying to fix the sink. I bent down beside him and asked him to let me do it. I was used to doing it and Paddy was never good at DIY. He threw the bucket he had beside him across the room and started screaming at me. He got up and went over to the kitchen door and kicked two planes of glass in the door, smashing them to bits. I got annoyed and shouted at him. He came back in and punched me in the mouth and told me I was a slut. The three kids were in the kitchen, hysterical. When he went to hit me again I ran at him and pushed him out into the hall. I wanted to try and get him away from the kids. I didn't push him hard enough to make him fall and he grabbed my throat. Outside the kitchen door, there was a cubby-hole under the stairs where we used to put the bikes. When he grabbed me by the throat he pushed me over the bikes and I really hurt myself. I didn't feel any pain and it was only when I went to the doctor the next day I found out that I had two broken ribs. The two eldest children dragged Paddy off me and the baby was yelling "Stop, dada, stop." I got up and made a lunge for him but he just lashed out and gave me a black eye. I think the screams of the children finally brought him to his senses and he stopped. He just went up to bed and I went into the kitchen and cried. They were tears of anger and frustration for being in such a position.

'The next morning when I woke, my eye was swollen and I was in a lot of pain. Paddy got up and when he came downstairs he was in great humour. We were usually terrified when he was getting up. His room was over the kitchen so we were able to hear what kind of humour he was in. If he got out of bed whistling, he was in good humour. If he got out of bed and banged things, he was in bad humour and I'd have to try and get the kids into the other room before he came down and warn them to stay away. The poor children were living with two monsters. They were in constant fear of mammy and daddy fighting. I was at the sink when Paddy came downstairs in great humour. I had his tea and toast on the table for him. I had to have his tea and toast waiting for him on the table when he came down because otherwise he would hit me. When I turned around from the sink he said "Jesus Christ, what happened to your eye?" When I told him that he had done it, he said that he never hit me. I asked my daughter to tell him what had happened and she told him that he had hit me. He told her that she was imagining things. After a while he actually had me asking myself "Did he really hit me?" He was in brilliant humour all day and kept asking me if I was all right. His behaviour was really freaking me out but I did my best to ignore him. I had to go to work the next day and when everyone asked me what had happened to my eye, I told them that I had walked into a door.

'Just after this particular beating, I got a letter from

the hospital marked urgent. It said that I was to get in touch with the hospital immediately. When I went to the hospital I was told that the cancer had returned and that it was necessary for me to have my womb removed. I went back home after being told this and I was very upset. When Paddy asked me what had happened I told him, I also told him that I wouldn't let them remove my womb. I felt that if they opened me up to take my womb out, then the cancer would spread. I tried to explain to him how I felt but all he said was "What's the point of keeping it. You'll never be any good as a woman anyway." That really hurt. He also used to call our son "the freak". When our son was born, he had a small problem with his genitals. When he was four he had an operation to rectify the problem. It used to hurt our son a lot when Paddy called him a freak. He is still only six.

'Christmas came and it was a horrible time. I borrowed £1,000 from the credit union to buy things for the kids and I started to gamble again. All over Christmas and the New Year we just didn't speak to each other. My job was just casual, and I had to work whenever I got the chance. There was a really big order to get out and for two weeks I worked from 8 am until 9 pm. I didn't see Paddy very much. When I got in I would just clean up and go to bed. He told the kids that I wasn't working, I was having an affair. When I came home at night, they would tell me that daddy was telling them that I was all sorts of horrible things. They were getting a really hard time from Paddy. I worked only for four weeks but it was very hard and I was very tired. For the last few days before I finished the job, I went to the pub at 9 pm because I didn't want to go home.

'By the following spring, I was at my wits' end. The tension in the house was terrible and it was like living with a time-bomb. I tried to fix Paddy's bike so that he would have an accident. I took the brake fluid out but I chickened out and told him that his bike was leaking. I used to pray each day that I would get a phone call to tell me Paddy was dead. He brainwashed the two eldest children. They began to take his side, which really made it hard for me. I had attempted suicide twice before and I knew that if I didn't do something, I couldn't go on. Three weeks ago I sat the children down and told them that I had to get out. I explained to them that if I didn't escape I would die. I knew that I couldn't take the kids because I had nowhere to go. I left the house for good on a Monday morning without a penny in my pocket. I left on the Monday because the week before had been terrible. Paddy had stopped giving me money and I was penniless. This was the last straw for me. I borrowed some money to tide me over the weekend and on Monday morning I left my home for the last time. I had no idea where I was going to go or what I was going to do. All I knew was that I had to get away. I went to the social services and they saw how upset I was. They rang a refuge for me and told me that there was a bed there for me. Now it was decision time. Knowing I was leaving I asked my eldest daughter if I was doing the right thing. She said to me: "Mammy, even if we only see you once a week, it's better than you being dead."

'Today is the first time I have seen the kids since I left and I am so happy. Paddy keeps telling the kids that I'll be back in three weeks. He thinks that because I have no money and nowhere to go I'll come home to him. He doesn't know me as well as he thinks he does. I am doing everything legally. That way when my case comes to court I'll have played by the rules. I have had no contact with Paddy since I left. The next time I see him will be in court. Now I am living only for my children. Without them I have nothing and my life has no purpose. I made the effort and broke free. Now all I want are my children.'

4
=

MARY'S STORY

Mary is twenty-eight years old and has two small children. It is eleven months since she left her violent partner and she is living in a refuge. She hopes to get a flat for her family in the near future.

'I had a very violent childhood. Me father was an alcoholic. Me ma always had black eyes but as a child I didn't understand. Da was always out drinking and when he got home there was always trouble. Ma used to call the gardaí, but by the time they arrived he'd be in bed so nothing ever happened. I remember the first time I ever got a cream cake. Da told me to do the washing up. Before I had finished I went to the toilet. When I came out of the toilet, me da hit me in the mouth with a knife, splitting my lip open. Ma was out at the shops, so he brought me out to Sandymount and bought me a cream cake so I wouldn't tell on him. A while after we moved to a new house. I came out of school one day and forgot my way to the new house so I went to our old house instead. Me nana was there and she took me home on her way to work.

When nana had gone he bashed me on the legs with the poker from the fire. It hurt for days. Da used to call us all in from playing at six o'clock every evening to say the Rosary. We all had to kneel and if any of us made a mistake saying our prayers he would batter us.

'He was always hitting me and I ran away from home a few times just to escape from beatings. I was always brought home and then I would get beaten for running away. Growing up, I thought that the time would never come when I could leave for good. When I did leave home for good, I went to England and it was there I met the father of my children. About three months after we met, I moved in with him. I became pregnant, but lost the baby when I was seven months pregnant. It was a girl. He battered me when I was pregnant, but said he was sorry. I believed him because he had never kicked me before and swore he would never hurt me again. After I lost the baby, I needed counselling but didn't get any. He wouldn't talk about it at all and things got worse. We decided to come back to Dublin. He stayed with his sister down the country and I stayed in me ma's. He used to hitch a lift to Dublin every weekend and it was like we were courting again and I was flattered with the attention. I needed him as well because I was taking panic attacks. I couldn't talk about the baby at home because da didn't allow us to show any emotion.

'I lived like this for nine months and then Joe (my boyfriend) and I got a flat. It was nothing fancy but at least we were together. I got pregnant two months after we moved into the flat, and Joe seemed to be pleased. I was looking forward to the baby, but I was worried that something might go wrong like the last time. The pregnancy went well and I gave birth to a healthy boy. I was only home from the hospital a week, when Joe battered me again for no reason. He had his hands around my throat and he was strangling me, I thought that I was going to die. I managed to grab an ashtray and hit him with it. I didn't hurt him, but it gave me time to break away from his grip and run out of the flat. I ran to the telephone box and dialled me ma's number, but before she answered I put the phone down. I decided that there was no point phoning her when there was nothing she could do. It would only upset her. I was walking back from the telephone box when my next-door neighbour stopped me. He asked me what was wrong and told me that they had heard the noise. He said that I could stay in his flat that night, so I did.

'When I went back to my own flat the next morning to get the baby and some clothes, Joe started crying. He told me that he was sorry for what had happened and that he would never do it again. I believed him yet again and stayed. He became very obsessive and followed me everywhere, even to the toilet. He was a really proud father when he was out with his mates but when he was at home it was a different story. If the baby cried at night he would tell me to get up and "feed that brat". We left the flat after about a year and moved to a house on the other side of town. I felt really isolated there and was thrilled when I bumped into a girl I had gone to school with who lived nearby. The only time I ever escaped was to do the shopping and even then I had to take Ciaran, my son. Joe asked me to have another baby, I thought to myself and decided that I would. The way I looked at it was I already had one and another one wouldn't make any difference. I had the baby, another boy, and when he was born Joe wouldn't believe that it was his baby. If I wanted to go out with my friend, I would have to pay Joe to babysit. One day he went out to the shops to buy some logs for the fire. He came back two days later. I could never ask Joe where he had been. He said that I had no right to ask about anything he did.

'Things got worse after our second child was born and Joe became more violent. He would tell me that all the trouble was my fault, it got to the stage that I could do nothing right. Joe got a job but all his wages went on drink. He never gave me any money. I found out that while the kids and I were at home starving, Joe was giving money to a girl in work because he felt sorry for her. She had left her husband. I was trying to survive on welfare payments of £52 per week. It got to the stage where I just couldn't take any more. When the baby was six months old, I left Joe and went back to me ma's. This wasn't an easy thing to do because I knew what it was going to be like at me ma's. I was under a lot of pressure and me da wasn't happy that we were staying there. I used to get up in the morning and leave the house with the kids at 9 am. I would stay out all day and come back when it was time to put the kids to bed.

'After about three months I had a big argument with da. He gave out because one of the children was crying and because Joe was ringing the house every hour. After the argument I knew that I had to take the kids and go. I left the house with the kids crying and walked to the bus stop. I really thought that someone from the house would follow me and tell me to come back, but no one did. I waited at the bus stop for a while and when no one came, I got the bus back to my own house. When I got home the house was all locked up. Joe was down the country with his sister. I smashed a window to get into the house, but when I got inside all the doors were locked. I spent two hours trying to drill through the kitchen door, to get in to make a bottle for the baby. Joe had phoned me ma's and knew that I was home. He came back the next day and I asked him to leave. He went without any trouble and I was in shock. About six weeks after he left, our youngest son needed to go into hospital for an operation. The day before the operation I stayed in me ma's. We had to be at the hospital very early and it was easier going from ma's. Joe called up to our house and when he saw that I wasn't there he phoned me mother's. Da said that I couldn't talk to him because I had gone to bed as I had to get up early the next morning. We were in the hospital when Joe arrived. He brought a big toy for Mark (our youngest son) and a tape of a love song for me. He was always trying to play on my heartstrings. He knew that he could play on the fact that he had grown up in a children's home and that I felt sorry for him because of this.

'As weeks went by he kept asking me to go back with him and when I said no he would accuse me of having an affair. He started pestering me and kept it up until I said that he could come and take the kids out. I thought that if I allowed him to see the kids then he would stop pestering me. When he called, supposedly to take the kids out, he would come into the house and stay there for the day picking on me. There was no escape from him. He tried to win the children over by buying them toys and sweets and promising them that it would be great when daddy came back to live. Eventually the pestering got worse and Joe got violent again. One day he came around and after I let him in, I went back into the kitchen to finish making the dinner. The kids were playing beside me as I was making the dinner. Suddenly Joe came into the kitchen in a temper and ripped the cooker away from the wall and threw it through the window. The kids were hysterical and as I tried to comfort them I screamed at Joe to get out. I told him that I hated him and I never wanted to see him again. He grabbed a knife and I thought he had slit his throat. There was blood everywhere and I thought he was dead.

'I grabbed the kids and ran out of the house, I ran all the way to my friend's house. I told my friend that I had to go back to my house to see if Joe was all right, at that moment I believed that he was dead. As I turned the corner leading into my road, I came face to face with Joe. He was covered in blood and he was swinging a big butcher's knife. He was screaming at the top of his voice that he was going to kill me. I just froze. I thought I was going to die. Luckily my friend had followed me from her house and she managed to get the knife out of Joe's hand. When he let go of the knife, he just walked away. My friend followed him to see where he was going but he just jumped on a bus. When I got back to my own house I discovered that he had been holding the knife the wrong way and had cut his hand. That was where all the blood had come from. When I went into the house with the kids the first thing we saw was blood everywhere. He had smeared blood all over the walls and the floor. I was trying to scrub the blood off the walls in the kitchen when suddenly Joe put his head through the broken window and said that he was sorry. I got an awful fright because I wasn't expecting him to come back again that day. I thought that he had gone home. I tried to think of how I could get the kids and run but before I knew it he was gone.

'I didn't sleep very well that night. I spent most of the time listening for him to return. He came back the following day and gave me money to get the window fixed. I told him that I wasn't going to stop him from seeing the kids but he wasn't going to come into the house again. He took the kids out twice and both times he came back really drunk. The second time he came back drunk I told him that I wasn't going to let him take the children out any more because I was afraid that something would happen to them. He just flipped and started battering me. He kept punching me and even the screams of the children didn't stop him. He left me in a heap on the floor and went around to my friend's house. He told her that he thought that he had broken my neck and asked her to go around and see how I was. When she arrived she told me to call the gardaí and have him charged but I was terrified that if I called the gardaí he would come back and kill me. Anyway, I had seen what had happened when me ma called the gardaí – nothing. So Joe got away with it once again.

'About a week after this, I woke up one morning to find

Joe standing at the end of my bed. The kids were sleeping in the bed with me so I didn't scream in case I woke them up. Joe said to me that he could have killed me and the kids and nobody would ever know. He had taken the locks off the windows and climbed in. Now I began to get really afraid, I knew that I wasn't safe even in my own home now. Every so often Joe would climb in when I was asleep. I would get up in the morning and find the cooker or the fire on. Joe did this to let me know that I wasn't safe and that I couldn't escape from him.

'I met another fellow who was married with kids of his own. He had already made up his mind to leave his wife before I met him. His wife used to slit her wrists in front of the kids and blackmail him all the time. It got to the stage where he couldn't take any more. When Joe found out that I was seeing another man he went mad. He went over to Jack's (my new fellow) house and smashed it up. Things got worse and Joe was calling up to me every week telling me that he loved me and wanted me back. The violence stopped for a while, I think he was trying to win me back. However, this didn't last long. I was on my way home one day when Joe met me at the end of the road. He got me by the hair and dragged me over to the river. When we got to the river he put my head under the water and tried to drown me. There was a man passing by who saw what Joe was doing and ran over to him and stopped him. Joe knew this man and when the man pulled him off me, he ran over to the his house and started trouble. Then Joe ran back to us. We were still sitting by the river. Joe said that he was going to kill me and the kids, that if he couldn't have us then nobody would. He ran across to my house and told the babysitter to get out. He grabbed a knife out of the drawer and taped it to a baseball bat. The gardaí caught him coming out of the house with the knife taped to the baseball bat in one hand and a cement block in the other hand.

'When the gardaí came over to me they asked me what the problem was. They said that Joe's face was in a very bad way. I explained to them that I had scratched his face when I was trying to stop him from drowning me. Joe told the gardaí that this was all my fault and that it was I who had attacked him. I pleaded with the gardaí to keep him in custody at least until the next morning to give me a chance to get away. They said that they couldn't and that Joe would be let go in an hour. I knew that I had to get the kids and run, I only had an hour to get what things I could and leave the house. I called Jack and he came over. He brought me and the kids to stay with friends. I stayed with these friends until I got a place in the refuge for the kids and me. I have been living in the refuge now for eleven months and I hope to be rehoused soon. When I am rehoused, Jack will move in with us. Joe still hangs around. He knows that I am at the refuge but he couldn't come near me here. He still sees the kids. He's all over them now. The younger fellow doesn't know him as daddy. I have had plenty of time to think in the past few months and one memory still haunts me. We were living in the flat in London at the time. Joe locked all the doors and put the key in his underpants. Then he came over to me and lifted me up. He took me to the balcony and hung me over it. We lived on the twelfth floor. He said that he would drop me over unless I was really nice to him. When he let me down I had to get the key.

'Jack is really nice, he is a normal guy. He knows what I've been through and understands. Joe put me through mental torture and physical abuse. I hope when I get a new place and Jack moves in, it will get Joe off the scene for good. At least now I won't have to try and cope with everything on my own, Jack will be there to help me. Please God my future will be better.'

5

CAROL'S STORY

Carol is forty-four, has one child and has been married and divorced twice. She is serving a two-year prison sentence for drug and fraud related crimes. Like 80 per cent plus of female prisoners, she is a victim of violence in the home. This is her story

'I had a very good upbringing – private schools, holidays and so on. My father died when I was twelve and when I was twenty, I went to London. I met a divorced man and fell madly in love. He told me that he had four kids – two were in care, the eldest was with his mother and the youngest with his ex-wife. I later found out that he had battered her too.

'I came back to Ireland and about six weeks later I discovered that I was pregnant. Mum made arrangements for me to go to my aunt in Liverpool and when my baby was born to have it adopted. I wasn't going to give my baby up, so instead I went to a mother and baby home where I stayed for about nine months. I saw Bill and showed him the baby – I had called her Mandy. Nine months after she was born I was offered a council flat. It was beside Bill's mother and he moved in with me.

'I was getting lone parent's allowance and he was getting dole. My money paid for everything and his money was for his drink. He would hit me regularly – always my left eye because he was right-handed. He was also mentally abusive, especially over me being Irish. I never screamed or shouted back. He ran up huge debts on mail order catalogues (he would sell the clothes) and he emptied the meters for drink money. The kids who were in care came to us for holidays. We got married in February 1976 and in January 1977 Bill's mother died. In the meantime we had been to court and had got custody of the children in care. All the time there were rows and fights – always when he came in drunk. I would know when there was going to be a fight because he would sit there staring at the television, but not seeing it. Then he would start hurling abuse at me and saying vile things. This would go on for hours. He then got an offer of a three-bedroomed house so he took it and I moved in with him. It was a nice house and I kept it clean. When his mother died, Bill's daughter who had been living with her grandmother, was very upset. We put in for another house and were offered a three-bedroom one which we refused. We wanted a four-bedroom house to accommodate all of us. We were offered another three-bedroom house but we refused that as well.

'Cathy, the eldest, had a part-time job. She used the money from this to buy herself clothes – it was her money. I gave the others pocket-money for doing jobs around the house. Cathy bought a T-shirt and sold it to a friend of mine for £1.50. My friend said that she would pay Cathy the following day. Bill went to collect his dole and saw my friend. He asked her for the £1.50 for the T-shirt and she gave it to him – he spent this on drink. I was really annoyed because this was money that Cathy had worked hard for, it wasn't my money, it was hers. I said this to him and he told me that Cathy was his daughter, not mine. Then he came at me and swiped me across the face with a potato peeler. I tried to retaliate but he went to town on me. I blacked out and he threw water over me to bring me to. I called the police because I was really frightened. They arrived and took me down to the station and took photographs of my injuries. They took me and the kids out of the house that night and brought us to an old folks' home until there was room at the battered wives' refuge.

'A couple of days later, an offer of a four-bedroom house was made and we decided that we would look at the house. I told the kids that if we went back to him, the next time I left I was going on my own. We took the house. Someone from Welfare collected me and Bill. Bill asked the Welfare guy if he would lend me his sunglasses while we went in to look at the house. We took the house and moved in. Bill promised that he wouldn't hit me again. This was in the summer. The rows were always worse at Christmas when I would spend money on the kids' clothes and presents. Bill was very jealous of the kids. He gave me a hand decorating but he'd get very irritated when something didn't go right the first time. The house was turning out well considering we were dependent on the dole.

'Lee, the eldest boy, was responsible for emptying the bin chute. If the chute wasn't closed properly the dogs would get at it and make a mess. One day Lee had been out all day and I knew that if he didn't come home and do the chute I would be on the receiving end of Bill's fist. Lee had thrown all the rubbish in the chute without closing it properly and the dogs had torn it to bits – there was rubbish everywhere. I knew that there would be trouble and I asked the eldest, Cathy, to go out and look for Bill and tell him to come home. When he came in, I told him that I couldn't cope and that I needed help. He told me that women should cope. There was a big fight and the kids jumped in for me. Afterwards he gave out to them for taking my side. The kids were very respectful of me and called me Mum. If there was money there, Bill would want to take me out if I had black eyes and show them off – he was proud of them.

'Coming up to Christmas, I would have to go with him when he collected his dole. Otherwise he'd spend most of it. He used to say that he was a 'steak man' and he would insist on meat every day. This was very hard because he would take a lot of money for drink and I had to try and manage on the small amount I had left. The kids and I would eat burgers while he had steak. I used to knit jumpers and tried to save some money for Christmas. I bought a Christmas tree and left it with my friend because I had a trolley and needed him to carry it. I had to wait up for him to come in that night – I could never go to bed if he was out because he would kick me out of the bed when he came in if I was asleep. He came in that night and started lashing out at me and kicking me about – I literally shit myself with fear. I called the police and they took him away. I was so scared I lay on the living-room floor all night afraid to go to bed. He came in a few hours later and told me to go to bed. He told me that the police were laughing at me. Whilst he was at the police station, I rang my mum and asked if I could come home. She said that I could but that I was only to bring Mandy (my own child). Anyway, he made me go to bed and insisted we have sex. I just lay there as if I was dead, I was so uptight I didn't know what else to do.

'That evening he searched my pockets and found money to go out for a drink. I had the shopping in for the week and I had bought the kids clothes and some toys. This was all they had. I knew that if I was to escape it had to be now. I took the bus fare to my friend's house from the milk money and Mandy and I went there. I rang my aunt and she said that she would give me the fare to come home to Ireland. All I had taken with me was my knitting and a jumpsuit for Mandy. Once before I had tried to run away and had all my stuff in the trolley. He got me and I paid for it. This time I had nothing but the clothes I stood in. I went to my mother with Mandy.

'Five months later, he came over to me and asked me to go back. He said that he couldn't cope without me – the gas and power had been disconnected and the kids would be taken into care if I didn't return. We ended up in bed, but I felt more secure because I was on home ground. He said that he had come over because he missed me and Mandy, but while he was here he didn't spend one penny on her. I knew that drink came before everything. I told him that I would stay one more week and think about it, but he wouldn't go until I said that I would go home. I went back and with the money I had saved from working, I had the power turned back on and bought the kids things. Everything was fine. He said that he would never hit me again. It was a year later when it started again. He got a job picking turnips. He didn't mind it but the other men did. I said that I would do it as this would be money for Christmas. I had also put in for a loan.

'One morning he wanted money for a paper. I had £13 in my pocket but I wouldn't let him know this. He would have wanted it all and this was my money for the children and for Christmas. I went up to have a bath and when I came down he said that he was going out. I didn't realise that he had taken some money until after I spent some myself. When I got in, he started on at me saying that I wouldn't give him the money for a lousy paper. It wasn't the money for the paper – he would have wanted it all. He started accusing me of doing filthy things with Lee, and I said to him that he must have seen this in his own home to say such a thing. He went mad and stormed out. When he came back he took the rest of the money and told me that if I didn't give it to him he would kill me. I had a chip pan on and he told me that he was going to melt my face with the oil. He went back out and I went down to my friend. I told her that I had had enough and that I wanted a divorce. I decided to go over and see my cousin who lived some miles away but she wasn't there so I returned home. The kids weren't there and I was frantic. I went back to my friend's to see if she could help and when I got there all the kids were with her. Cathy told me that Bill told her that if I wasn't back by the time he got home, he was going to give her what I should be getting. Cathy got the kids and ran to my friend's – they were all terrified. I applied for and subsequently got a divorce.

'Bill didn't want a divorce so to get him to sign the papers, I took him to bed and told him he could have sex if he signed the papers. He did sign the papers – in bed. I told him that I would stop the divorce if we got another house. He saw his solicitor who told him that I was lying (which I was). He came looking for me and wanted to sleep with me. He said that he'd say we slept together, so I said I'd sleep with him if he didn't say this. The divorce came through a short time later – exactly four years after we married.

'I settled down to life without him, I had got custody of the four kids after the divorce because they didn't want to go with him. I got a good job in the civil service and I also had a part-time job at night. I was financially stable, had lost weight I needed to lose, dressed nicely and went out. The kids and I lived well for the first time in a long time. I started my new job in the civil service in April. Life was good.

'In August, Bill asked me to go to a wedding with him. I agreed and went out of my way to look good that day. I suppose I wanted to show him how well I was managing without him. We went to the wedding and at the reception that night, he left me, saying that he was going to change. I was up dancing when he came back and he got very annoyed and punched me. I went to leave but he dragged me back, I couldn't get away from him. At the end of the night, he came out with me and I told him that I was going home. He dragged me down the road and then took my handbag, emptied it and threw it away. When we got to my house I couldn't open the door because he had thrown my keys away. Bill kicked the front door in and when the kids came down to see what was happening he told them to get lost and to get into the sitting-room and not to move. He then dragged me up the stairs and raped me. He left the next morning after apologising for what he had done. The kids had sat up all night afraid to go to bed because he had told them not to move. I was covered in bruises and very badly shaken – as were the kids.

'I was seeing a new man and I told him about what Bill had done. He said that I must go to the police or it would keep happening. I realised that he was right, so I did. I told them what I knew – where he lived, drank and so on. They told me that I couldn't get a Barring Order because he didn't live in the area (he lived in London and I was still in Liverpool). That was the end of that. Time went on and I met another guy, Sam. We started living together and a short time later we got married. It wasn't working out with him and the kids. He wasn't helping. I used to get in from one job and in the hour I was at home before leaving for my other job, I had to make the dinner and do everything. It was one mad rush and he didn't seem to care. I tried to be fair with the kids but I could never seem to get it right with Lee. If I bought him something it would never be what he wanted and he never had enough. I would leave our bus fares in piles. There would be five fares left on the table and when I went to get my bus fare it would be gone. Things were getting too much for me and Lee was getting too difficult to manage. Lisa (the daughter who was in care) started acting up. I asked Bill's brother if he would take Lee to live with him. I asked Sam to take Lee to my brother-in-law's and he said that he thought he should leave as well. I didn't object, I wanted a peaceful life. Lee left and Sam left – we had been married six weeks and had known each other only six weeks before we married. With them gone, there was only me and the three girls in the house. The atmosphere got very bad. Lisa had left school and was working. Cathy and Lisa contributed with Cathy paying the rent (£4) and Lisa paying the instalments for a new suite of furniture (£3). I still had two jobs. My main job paid the housekeeping and the second job was for luxuries, I was saving for us to go on a holiday to Butlins.

'When Bill found out that Lee had left, he phoned me from London and started screaming abuse down the phone at me, then he hung up. Lisa had got in with a bad crowd and got caught shoplifting. Mandy was with her. I went to the station and got them. The next morning, I went to court and pleaded for Lisa. She was released. I went to work and she went home.

'That afternoon, Bill came up from London and called to the house. Lisa let him in and he cleared the house from top to bottom. He took absolutely everything – all he left was the cooker. When I got home I couldn't believe it, I called the police to report it and they said it was a domestic. I asked them how could they say it was a domestic when I wasn't even married or living with the man. His two girls told the police that I had been fiddling the electric and showed them how. I was arrested – this was the first time I had been charged.

'This betrayal of trust by his girls was the last straw. I rang my mother and asked her if I could come home but she said that she wouldn't be able for me around the house. I took Wendy and went to London, I worked there for two years. I was very worried because I was claiming benefit and working at the same time. I asked Mandy, who was now eleven, did she want to live in France or in Ireland. She said that she couldn't speak French so she picked Ireland. We came to Ireland and I was home.

'About a year-and-a-half later, I heard that Lee had committed suicide. I felt very guilty – that we all had a part to play in his suicide. I had taken responsibility for him and I was the only mother he had ever known. This is when I started taking drugs. Without drugs I would have been dead a long time ago.

'With the drugs and crime I did everything I wanted to do. I went to Disneyland with Mandy, bought a fur coat, bought a new house and lived a good life. I had planned to get a job and save for all these things when I first came and when I couldn't get a job, I turned to crime.

'I sent Mandy to a private school and she did well in her Leaving. I paid for a computer course and she went to London in 1992. She stayed with Bill for a while but things didn't work out – he was accusing her of sleeping with her step-brothers.

'About a year ago I met a man and he's the only one I have had a true relationship with since Bill. Mandy loves him and he's a kind and loving man. We live together. I don't know what the future will hold for me. I have no support from my family and that hurts. I don't think about how my life might have been and I don't think about how I wanted my life to be. I turned to drugs in a dark moment and I turned to crime to survive. I don't think I'm a bad person and I've never hurt anyone. I've always tried to provide for my children and in the end, my best just wasn't good enough. I don't know what the future holds, but I do know it can't be worse than my past . . . '

TENDER

Married life can be warm and tender
Until your husband goes on a bender,
When he gets home to the boxing ring,
The rounds with you make him feel king.
He rants and raves about nothing at all,
If you answer it's like talking to the wall,
You sit and listen, saying yes and no,
Hoping your answers are right whatever way you go.
When the shouting and screaming is over,
He rises quick to have his fun,
The hair is first, to drop you quick.
A dig in the mouth, a burst lip.
Please oh! Please you shout in pain,
You realise your pleas are in vain,
Two panda eyes for all to view,
Does he believe he's been crowned anew.
Then like a matador he's in for the kill,
Kicking and punching till your nose overspills,
With the gore all over your face,
He gets a damp cloth to wipe away the trace.
Oh how the remorse sets in bad,
What have I done, I'm sorry for getting mad,
Up to the bedroom let me hold you tight,
For what – to love and kiss you better all night.

Victim of Abuse, September 1994

6

ALICE'S STORY

Alice is nineteen, has a two-year-old daughter in care, is single and still lives at home. Alice is serving a custodial sentence for assault and attributes this to suffering at the hands of an abusive mother. This is her story.

'My mother used to beat me with shovels and brushes – I never knew why she beat me. She started beating me when I was about nine and she used to say to me that if I told my father she would kill me. I was too afraid to ever tell anyone about it.

'Once when I was about eleven, she stuck a meat fork in my leg. I couldn't walk for nearly two months. I was lying in bed for nearly two months and she wouldn't let me see a doctor. My father saw me and brought me to a doctor. I was so happy that he knew at last. He and my mother fought about this for a long time. There was never any violence between my mother and father – they would fight all the time, but they would tell us to get out while they were fighting. My dad would leave and then my mother would shout at us all when he left. I often wondered why it was only me she picked on – I had four sisters and four brothers and they all lived at home except one brother.

'Once she hit me so hard, I was in bed for four months. I couldn't move my arm and she used to come up with food once a day and throw it on the floor so that I would have to pick it up. I never did anything to make her annoyed but she still beat me. It was never only a smack – she always hit to hurt and injure.

'My father committed suicide four years ago and she blames me for his death. I actually saw my father kill himself – he jumped off a bridge. He gave me money that morning to buy myself a pair of jeans. I was getting off the bus to go home when I saw crowds of people at the bridge. I went over and was wondering what had happened, then I saw that everyone was looking at my father who had just jumped to his death off the bridge. I was in total shock and couldn't believe what I was seeing.

'My mother has been drinking heavily since my father died. She's also on tablets for her nerves. She's not bad all of the time, but when she is bad we all leave the house for a while. We're afraid of her, to be honest. My mother's not well now – she's sick.

'I think that it is because of her I am the way I am. She's the one who has ruined my life and I think that is why I assault people – the gardai mainly. I know why I do it, I just feel that I have to lash out. My mind is so messed up. I put my daughter into care. I have no contact with her. I blame my mother for everything she's done to me. I was only a child and I couldn't fight back.

'I'll always love her – but I'll never forgive her for what

she did to me and the pain she has caused me. I will never ever understand why she did it to her own child. I would love to settle down and be happy. Maybe some day I will . . . '

7

JOANNE'S STORY

Joanne is thirty, separated and has three children. One
child lives with her boyfriend's mother and the other two
children are in care. Joanne is a heroin addict and is HIV
positive. She is currently serving a ten-month sentence for
larceny. From the age of thirteen, Joanne was a victim of
physical and mental abuse in the home. This is her story.

'I was with my husband since I was thirteen. I was only
fourteen when I had my first child, a girl. He was always
jealous and possessive. He used to say the baby wasn't
his. I was with him the day before he went to court and
he got nine months. When he came out he was good to
the baby and wanted us to get married. I kind of went
along with it all. Him, my ma and his ma paid for everything and arranged everything. I squatted with the baby
in a flat on me ma's balcony and did the whole flat up
myself. He would come in and a row would start usually
over drinking. There would be murder. One night he came
in and wrecked the flat. I mean wrecked the flat so I
couldn't live in it. I had to go and live with my mother

and he knew that I couldn't apply for a barring order from my mother's flat. He settled a bit after this but still drank. He got a job.

'I started on drugs when I was fifteen and the baby was two months old. He drank and I took drugs. I got off the drugs in de-tox and was off them for a while. I was sixteen when all the plans for the wedding were being made. I wanted to stop it but I couldn't. I didn't even pick my wedding dress. On the morning of my wedding I knew that I couldn't live with him and didn't want to marry him. I thought of how he had put me in hospital after a beating when I was fifteen. I had broken ribs.

'Anyway, because we didn't have a house, on the morning of the wedding people called and gave me money in envelopes. I took the envelopes and put them in my pocket. A while later I left the house and went to the flat of a fella who sold drugs. I had £750 in my pocket. This fella didn't know that I was supposed to be getting married that day, and I just sat in his flat banging up. I wanted to die rather than get married. A friend who was coming to the wedding arrived at the flat to buy some gear and saw me sitting there. He said that I had to get home and get ready. No taxi wanted to take me, but he finally gave a bloke money to bring me home. It was 3.40 pm when I got home, I was supposed to have been at the church at 3pm. I was in a bad way and they had to dress me. The car arrived and brought me to the church. The fella who was giving me away had to carry me up the aisle, I was so drugged I couldn't reply to the priest. I woke up in Blackpool two days later and I had seven quarters in my bra. When I woke up I had no works, no syringe or anything. I went downstairs and asked a man for directions to a chemist. I went to the chemist and got what I needed, then I went back to the hotel and asked when the next flight to Dublin was. I booked out of the hotel and went home. I didn't see my husband at all.

'He rang my ma and said he was going to kill me. I told my ma that I was trying to overdose because I didn't want to get married. She said that I should have told her. Now I know I should have. He stayed on in Blackpool for the time we had been booked for, and when he came back I told him that I didn't want to be married. He said that I *was* married and there was nothing I could do about it now. I lived in my ma's and he lived with his ma. We were offered a house and we took it. As soon as we moved I knew it was a mistake. I was away from all my family and my ma. He used to go missing for days. His sister who lived near us told me to leave him. Eventually I did because of all the hidings. During one bad row I stabbed him twice and he went to the hospital. I couldn't have given a shit if he died. What made me leave in the end was that he went to collect his labour and went missing for two days. I got all the locks changed and when he came back I wouldn't let him in. He went and got petrol and poured it in the letterbox. Then he lit a match, threw it in and ran away. The hall went up, I got the baby and escaped out the back. I was really annoyed because the baby's room was right above the hall and he could have killed her.

'Two days later, I went in to give back the keys of the house. When I arrived, he had all my clothes in a pile in the back garden and they were burning. I went back to my ma's with the baby. My ma got a barring order because it was her flat. He broke it a few times and my ma didn't report him. I told her that he would keep hassling us unless she got him done. When she did report him, he got six months. I was eighteen then.

'When he got out of prison, he came to the pub I was in and got me outside. Then he broke a bottle off the wall and slashed my face. The people in the pub called an ambulance and I was taken to hospital. I told them in the hospital not to ring the gardai because I knew that if they did, he would probably go to prison and would kill me when he got out. I went over to my cousins and told them what had happened. They gave him some gangsters' beating. They told him that if he ever came near me or the baby again they would kill him. He knew that they weren't messing and he did stay away from me. I met a new bloke and he's great. I don't get punched around any longer . . . '

8

PAT'S STORY

Pat is twenty-two, single, has a three-year-old and is responsible for her sister's eleven-year-old son. She is currently serving a six-month sentence for larceny. She is HIV positive and still in an abusive relationship. This is her story.

'When I was twelve, my mother and father died within six months of each other, my mother of cancer and my father from a heart attack. When they died, those who had been away from home came back to live in the house again. We all lived together as a family for a few months. A few months later my eldest sister left and then they all started leaving. There were eight of us and I came second last. Two of my sisters died within a year of each other, one from a hit-and-run accident and one from AIDS. I'll tell you about my sister who died from AIDS later.

'We were never really a close family. I couldn't tell anyone when I got my periods when I was twelve. I was afraid to tell so I used to save up to buy sanitary towels. Anyway, when my eldest sister moved out, she took my little sister to live with her. That left only me, my sister and brother in the house. Joan got sent to prison and when she got out, she put her son who was two, into care. She stayed in England for only about five months and when she came back, she took her son out of care and got a flat. This left me and my brother in the house. The electricity had been cut off, so I went to live with Joan. I went back to the house a few months later and it was a tip. My brother was just using it as a place to have drinking sessions. Shortly after this the house was boarded up. My brother is married with three kids now and he is HIV.

'I moved in with Joan when I was fifteen and I met Phil, my present fella. He was security for me – he bought me things and brought me out. Nobody had done that for me before. Two years later my sister was killed by a hit-and-run driver. She had three young children. She and Joan were very close and when she was killed it was as if Joan gave up the will to live. She died of AIDS less than a year later, leaving a seven-year-old son behind. I was eighteen and two weeks pregnant when she died.

'I got her flat because of her son and I carried on living there and looked after Shane as if he were my own. A girl moved into another flat on the same floor as me. She was a drug-pusher and that's when I started taking drugs. She was giving me drugs for about a year in exchange for my holding drugs in my flat. Phil never touched heroin until he met me; he just drank heavily. I used drugs when I was pregnant because I had gallstones and when the pain came, I would take drugs to block it out.

'I haven't slept with Phil in the past year, I don't like him to touch me any longer. He says that I'm sleeping around but this is not true. I don't go out, Phil is the only boyfriend I have ever had and the only man I ever slept with in seven years. Phil has been very violent to me in the past year or so. I want him to go but I'm afraid to tell him how I really feel. He's obsessed with me and once said to me that if I ever left him, he would destroy my face. I knew he wasn't messing with me.

'I had to start going out robbing to feed our habit. Phil stayed with the kids while I went out. He didn't want to do this, but I wasn't going to bring the kids robbing with me. It would have a bad effect on them. He keeps throwing this in my face. He says that everyone is saying that he is living off me. He is sure that whatever he thinks is true and I can't change his mind.

'When I was three months pregnant he said that he baby wasn't his and he tried to kick it out of me. I had been to a dance and he was waiting for me when I got home. He was drunk and I'll never forget the beating he gave me. My face, neck and eyes were black and blue. He told everyone he left me because the baby wasn't his. Coming back killed him because he had to admit he'd lied. He said that he did it because he loved me.

'The only way I can fight is with words. If he hits me, I tell him that he's not a man – that drives him mad. His mother was there once when he gave me a beating. He wouldn't stop punching me and when his mother tried to protect me, he picked up a heavy glass astray and kept smashing it off my shins.

'I met a girl the last time I was in prison who was gay. I got very close to her but we didn't sleep together. She came up to the house a few times after we got out. Phil was asking everyone was I gay and was this why I didn't love him. This other girl wants to be with me, but she knows Phil is in the way. She doesn't want to cause any trouble for me.

'A week before I came in Phil went to a christening. When he came home I was asleep – it must have been about one in the morning. Earlier I had given a friend a loan of his bike. He started screaming at me and asking where his bike was. He was going mad around the flat with a knife in his hand. He came over to me and told me to get out, I said that I was tired and was going to bed. He came after me and put the knife to my throat. He made me sit back on the bed, then he pushed me down. The knife was at my throat all the time. I felt so helpless. He said he was sorry the next morning and I just told him to get out. He looked me straight in the eye and said that he would never leave me.

'The night before I came in, I fell asleep on the sofa. He came in beside me and I told him to stay away from me. He asked me was I gay. I couldn't answer him, I'm so confused. I would be so happy if Phil left. I've gone to prison twice just to get away from him. He makes me sick sometimes and he talks to me as if I'm nothing. He often batters me in front of the kids. The three-year-old clings to me and the eleven-year-old goes hysterical. After he batters me, he just sits down as if it's all forgotten about and tells me to go and buy him some beer.

'The morning I was in court, he made me go into the kitchen and cook breakfast, then he made me dress the kids and clean up. I was finished doing this at 10.20 am (I should have been in court at ten o'clock). He made sure

I was late because I wouldn't have sex with him the night before. I haven't seen him since.

'I truly hate him. He's driven me to the the state I am in today – I have no interest whatsoever in men. He knows that I have no one but the kids and he says that if I ever left him, I would never see the baby again. He's caused so much trouble over nothing and has been calling me so many things for so many years. He has me so confused. This girl made me believe that I was someone. I confided in her and she listened. She cared, and would say to me "Just leave him." He'll never leave and he has my life in bits. I was too young when I went out with him and stayed with him for all the wrong reasons.

'I'd love him to leave, I'd love to be free of him but I have two children to think about and I know that if I ever tried to leave or have him thrown out, he'd kill me or leave me wishing I was dead. What do I see for the future? I don't have a future.'

9

SHARON'S STORY

Sharon is in her late fifties and lives in the north of Ireland. She is married and has a son in his twenties. For the past eight years she has been a victim of violence in the home. The abuser is her own son. Her husband, family and friends know nothing of the abuse and Sharon wants it that way. This is her story.

'Greg was a very welcome baby. My husband and I had been trying for a baby for five years before I got pregnant, and when I did, there couldn't have been a happier expectant mother than me. I enjoyed every minute of my pregnancy and when Greg was born and the nurse handed him to me, I knew that I would spend the rest of my life loving this baby. Greg was a very good baby, always smiling and cheerful. I had no regrets about not returning to work, so that I could watch him growing up. My heart broke in two the day he started school. He looked so grown up in his uniform and he was so happy to be going to "big school". He charged into the classroom and immediately began talking to a group of children. When I went to kiss him goodbye, he turned to me and said "I'm a big boy now." He was so busy playing he didn't even notice me leaving the classroom.

'Greg's early years in school passed quickly and he had lots of friends. His report cards always remarked how polite and well-mannered he was, and his grades were good as well. Greg was a very kind little boy – he used to call into our elderly next-door neighbour to keep her company and cut her grass. He had a paper round and would save for weeks to buy me something nice for my birthday or Christmas or whatever the occasion was. Our house was festooned with things he brought home from school, and as the years passed, the box where I put all the cards he gave me was over-flowing. Greg and his dad would go swimming every week and they often went away camping. Greg used to joke with me when I asked could I go camping with them. He'd say that I was too afraid of spiders to sleep outdoors.

'Greg was a popular boy and his friends were always in the house. His friends were a nice group of boys and there was never any trouble. We gave Greg his freedom and in return we asked that he didn't abuse it. If he went out, he told us where he was going and what time he'd be back. We could trust him. At fourteen it was hard to know just how much freedom to give him. In the end we just went by what his friends were allowed to do. We would have one night a week put by for a 'family night'. We all enjoyed this and it gave us a chance to talk to him about things. We were very close and Greg knew that he could talk to us about anything. When he took an interest in a girl when he was fourteen, he and I stayed up talking until two in the morning. He asked me what was the best way to get her to notice him. It took me all my time to keep a straight face during much of our conversation, but I was glad that he felt he could confide in me. It was shortly after this my husband got a promotion in work which meant that we would have to move house. At first Greg wasn't too happy about this and moaned about having to leave all his friends and school. We reasoned with him that it was going to be hard for all of us but we would soon make new friends and get settled.

'The new house was lovely and Greg was delighted that there were so many things to do. He joined the local youth club and karate club and made friends quickly. He settled in well at his new school and his grades were comparable with previous reports. I got a part-time job and for a year things couldn't have been better. It was a little over a year after we first moved that I began to notice a change in Greg. For a while, it was something that I couldn't quite put my finger on. He began staying out without telling us where he was going and when we grounded him he refused to come out of his room. He was getting very cheeky and began answering me back a lot. I noticed that he only did this when his father was not around. When Jack was there, Greg would be as nice as pie. Jack's job meant that he would be away from home for a week every month, sometimes more. I know that I began to dread Jack being away.

'The first time I noticed that money was missing from my purse was at the check-out in the local supermarket. I had been to the bank the day before and I knew that I had £100 in my purse. My shopping came to £65 and when

I went to get the money out of my purse there was only £60 there. I had to write a cheque to pay for my shopping and drove home in a daze. So many things were going through my mind that I almost crashed the car. A nagging voice inside my head kept telling me what had happened the money but I refused to believe it. I couldn't accept that Greg would steal from me. I convinced myself that there was some perfectly logical explanation for the money missing. When I got home, I left the groceries in the bags on the kitchen floor and made myself a cup of tea. I went into the lounge and sat down at the chair beside the fire. So many things were going through my mind and it was hard to think rationally, when every time I looked up, I saw smiling photographs of Greg as a baby and toddler,

'Gradually I faced the fact that Greg was the only person who had access to my handbag. Greg had come home in very bad humour the night before and when I asked him what was wrong he told me to leave him alone. I tried talking to him again. I told him that he could talk to me and together we could work anything out. He replied that if I didn't leave him alone, he was going to go out and he wouldn't come back. I decided that the best thing I could do was to leave him alone so I went upstairs to my bedroom. I listened carefully to make sure that he didn't go out and when I finally heard him go to bed, I fell asleep. My handbag was downstairs.

'As I sat in the lounge thinking of all this, I knew that I would have to confront Greg but I wasn't sure how. I decided that I would tell him about what happened in the supermarket and see what his reaction was. As I waited for him to come home, I remembered a couple of times during the previous weeks that I thought I had more money than was in my purse.

'It was after ten that night when Greg finally came home from school. I told him that I wanted to talk to him. We sat down at the kitchen table and I asked him directly why had he taken the money. He said that I had over £100 in my purse and that he thought I could afford to give him £40. I was so shocked at his reaction that I was speechless. I told him that if he ever did anything like that ever again, I would tell his father and call the gardai. I was trying to frighten him and fully expected him to tell me he was sorry and would never do it again. Instead he turned into a madman. Still sitting, he upturned the kitchen table, sending everything on it smashing to the ground. Then he got up and smashed the chair he was sitting on against a work-top. I was too terrified to move and just kept screaming at him to stop. He seemed to listen to me and stopped. There was silence and then he came over to me and started crying. He told me that he hadn't meant to do what he had done and told me he was sorry for taking the money. With the table upturned and broken glass everywhere, he knelt with his head in my lap and we talked. I asked him what was so wrong that he was driven to this and he told me that he had some problems but he couldn't tell me about them. I asked him was he in trouble with anyone and he said no. He said that he would sort it out and I pleaded with him to let me help. He asked me not to tell his father what had just happened or about his problems and I said that I wouldn't. He told me that if I ever told his father, he would pack his bags and leave and I would never see him again. We cleared up the mess and I stuck the chair back together again. Greg went to bed and I sat in the kitchen for a very long time. I knew that he was in trouble and I wanted to help. I didn't know what kind of trouble he was in but put it down to pressure of his exams which were coming up in a few weeks. I sat there in the darkness with tears streaming down my face, unable to believe that this was the same little boy who used to tell me that I was the most loveliest mummy in the whole world. I felt very isolated, knowing that I couldn't talk to anyone about him in case he found out.

'Greg seemed to make an effort after the outburst. He came home from school most days and seemed to be studying hard. I noticed that when he did go out, he could come back in great humour. This went on until after his exams, a few weeks later. For those few weeks it was like the 'old' Greg was back. He was much quieter but made an effort to be civil. After discussing the subject of his allowance with Jack, we decided to increase it by £10 per week. I thought that this might help him. He always seemed to be short of money even after getting this increase, and quite a few times I heard him ask Jack for money. When the results of the exams came out and Greg did not achieve the marks he needed to attend university, he seemed to stop trying again. He wouldn't talk to me and I was seeing a side of him that my husband knew nothing about. Jack was going away more often now and Greg seemed to think that he could do what he liked when his father was away. He began hanging around with a group of lads who weren't very nice. The only reason I knew about this was that a neighbour told me because she felt I ought to know. When I asked Greg about this, he said that it was none of my business who he saw and there was nothing I could do about it. I told him that I would tell his father and he said that if I knew what was good for me I wouldn't.

'I couldn't believe the type of person Greg had become. Most of the time he acted as if he hated me. I knew that it was just a phase he was going through and each night I prayed that he would return to his old self. With his father away more often now, Greg began being abusive to me. Once he asked me for some money and when I said that I didn't have any, he emptied the contents of my handbag on the floor to search for money. When he couldn't find any, he got me by the hair and told me to tell him where it was because he needed it a hell of a lot more than I did. I had money put by to pay some bills, so I gave it to him. When he put it in his pocket, he turned to me and said 'Mum, why do you make me hurt you when I love you so much?'

'Again I asked him to tell me what was wrong and again he said that he couldn't. He said that he needed the money to get him out of a spot of bother. As he left he said that he wouldn't be home that night. When I asked him where he was going he said "Away". I asked him not to go and he said that after what he had done he thought that I would want him out and that anyway his father would kill him for what he had done to me. I told him that I would always love him no matter what and that I wouldn't tell his father. He said that he wouldn't leave.

'I loved him so much and I was afraid that if he left

home, he would do something really stupid to get money. At least if he was at home the only person he could harm was me and I wasn't going to have him sent to jail. I also knew that it was only a phase he was going through and sooner or later he would be back to his old self.

'Despite myself and Jack talking to him, Greg decided that he wasn't going to repeat his exams and that he didn't want to go to university. This broke our hearts, but we weren't going to force him to do something he didn't want to do. Jack got him a job and Greg seemed to like it. For a while everything was fine until Greg decided that the office was too far away and he wanted a job closer to home. I tried to explain to him that jobs weren't easy to come by and Greg replied that he might go to England to find work. My heart missed a beat when he said this, so I told him I would try and help him until he found another job closer to home. I wanted to say to him that a thirty-minute journey wasn't far but I was afraid to. A couple of months later, Jack found out that Greg had been sacked because he was always missing days and most of the days he did go into the office, he was either very late or left very early.

'Greg didn't really look for another job. I'd buy the paper and mark jobs I thought would be suitable but he wouldn't even look at the ones I'd marked. When Jack was around, Greg would ring jobs and set up interviews but what Jack didn't know was that Greg would never turn up for the interviews. Many times there would be a phone call asking where Greg was because he was supposed to be attending an interview and there was no sign of him. He was getting moodier by the day and the tension was terrible. Jack was away on business more often and I was finding it harder to cope with Greg. If I'm honest, I was afraid of Greg. I was afraid of his violent outbursts and it was getting harder to hide the evidence of them. Once my next-door neighbour knocked on my door to ask was everything all right. She had heard Greg screaming at me and heard things being smashed. I told her that everything was just fine and that Greg and I were just having a disagreement, I'll never forget the look she gave me. She knew that I was lying but didn't say it to me. She did ask me if Jack was there and I told her that he was away. I had to go into her the next day and ask her not to mention anything to Jack. I told her that Greg was under a lot of pressure and my nagging had only made it worse and that he has snapped. Greg went into her later to apologise for disturbing her and to assure her that it was only a once-off argument. She accepted our explanation and there was never another mention of it again.

'I had to hide any money I had in the house and I tried to have as little cash as possible. Once Greg even took the milk money.

'I know you are probably saying to yourself, why didn't she just phone the gardai or tell her husband or kick him out, I've asked myself the same thing. Deep down though I know the answer. I love my son and I know that the person he has become is not the person he really is, I know that he doesn't want to do the things he is doing. Anytime there is an outburst, afterwards he cries and tells me he's sorry. It's not his fault – I think that at times he is as scared as I am. I found out the reason for his behaviour in a very frightening way.

'Jack was away working and Greg had been asking me for money all day. He kept saying to me that it was a matter of life or death and I was telling him not to be so dramatic. He told me that he had to have the money that night – otherwise he'd be in trouble. When I asked him to tell me what was wrong, he told me that he didn't want to involve me in his problems. He was being very aggressive and ripped the telephone out of the socket when I threatened to call the gardaí. I was frightened when he did this because I knew that now there was no way for me to contact anyone if I needed help. I was determined that there was no way I was giving him money and I told him that he could beat me to a pulp, but I still wasn't handing him money. All I had in my purse was four pounds and I told him this. After a while, he stopped asking me for money and became very quiet. He wouldn't tell me what was wrong. All he kept saying to me was "I told you I needed the money; I told you it was important." I cleaned up the place and got on with some ironing. A couple of hours later there was a knock on the door. Greg went white and told me not to open it – he looked really scared. I told him not to be silly and said that if the caller was for him I would tell them that he was out.

'When I answered the door there were two well-dressed men standing there. They asked me if they could speak to Greg and I told them that he wasn't in. One of the men said that they knew he was there and ushered me inside, closing the door behind them. I screamed and they told me to shut up and get Greg. Greg came out into the hall and told them to leave me alone. I couldn't believe that Greg knew such people. They asked Greg why he had not turned up as arranged and he told them that he didn't have their money. They asked him why the phone had been engaged for hours and before Greg had a chance to answer, I said that I had been on the phone to my sister – I didn't want them to know that the phone wasn't working. They told Greg that they had warned him what would happen if he didn't have the money. It was only then it dawned on me – all the mood-swings, the desperation for money, the depression and all the other signs. Greg was using drugs. I felt so stupid for not realising this before now, I felt that I had failed him as a mother. I should have known, I should have been able to help. I'd say all of this went through my mind in about twenty seconds.

'I knew that these men wouldn't take no for an answer and all of a sudden my fear vanished. All they wanted was their money, I just had to make sure they got it. I looked at Greg, who was standing there ashen-faced, I knew that he didn't want this to happen and I knew that he wasn't a hardened criminal either.

'Without even looking at Greg, I asked the men how much he owed them. They told me it was £200 and they wanted it now. I asked them to take my word that they would get it and asked them to call back in an hour. I explained that I had no money in the house and that I would go and get it from the bank machine. I said that I wasn't going to mess them around and that the money would be there when they came back. They left after telling me what they were going to do if the money wasn't there when they returned. When they left my legs gave way and Greg helped me up – we were both crying. Greg said that he never meant for me to find out and he never meant for me to get involved. He explained that once he got involved with drugs he couldn't stop. He said that he was so desperate for drugs, he'd do anything to get them. After he hurt me he said he would cry himself to sleep. I believed him, I'd read about drugs and how they take over a person's life. He came with me and waited while I withdrew the money. We went home and waited for the men to return. When I gave them the money, they actually apologised for upsetting me and explained that they had to make a living too. They assured me that they would never both me again, unless of course Greg owed them money.

'That night, Greg and I stayed up the whole night talking. I said to him that I couldn't take any more, I told him that I would have to tell his father or the gardaí about what had happened. He begged me not to, he said that he couldn't face living any more if I didn't. He swore that he would stop and asked me to help him.

'The first thing we did was go to a rehabilitation centre. Greg attended all the sessions and although it wasn't easy, he came off drugs and made a fresh start. He got a job and was even doing a night course. I never told Jack about what had happened and as the months progressed and Greg stayed on the straight and narrow, I convinced myself that I had done the right thing. It must have been about a year later that Greg decided that he was going to get his own flat, he said that he felt he was ready to stand on his own two feet. Although I didn't want him to go, I knew that I mustn't try to stop him by being selfish.

'The house was very quiet when Greg moved out, and

I missed him most when Jack was away. He did visit often and I did his washing for him. He seemed very happy and I was glad that things had worked out so well. Six months after he moved out, he called around and asked me for money on the pretext that it was to pay a gas bill. I told him that I couldn't give him any money, but, if he brought the bill to me I would go in and pay it for him. He was really annoyed and stormed out. I was worried sick that he had started using drugs again and called to his flat. There was no answer so I left a note for him. It was two weeks before I heard from him again even though I had left over a dozen messages for him to ring home. When he eventually called he said that he had been busy, I asked him was everything OK. He said that it was and asked if he could call around. I told him that he didn't need to ask if he could call around, it was after all his home. He called later that evening and demanded money. He tore the house upside down looking for money. I gave him everything I had and told him to go before I called the gardaí. I couldn't believe that after all he had put me through he was doing this again. I wanted to call the gardaí, but I just couldn't. I didn't want to get him into trouble and ruin his life. A couple of days later I got a letter from him – it said that by the time I would read the letter he would be gone and out of my life forever. He said that he was sorry for hurting me and that if he wasn't near me then he couldn't hurt me. He explained that he couldn't help what he was doing and asked me not to tell his father about anything. I cried until I couldn't cry any more. What I most feared had happened. I felt that he had let me down by running away, I felt angry because he had already hurt me so much and now he was hurting me again. Most of all I felt as if I had lost my son.

'Over the next couple of years, he wrote and phoned, but the letters were always short and the conversations short. At times it was like talking to a stranger. Everytime he contacted me, I asked him to come home and let me help him. He said that it was his life and this was the way he chose to live it. He came home for a few days a few times, and listening to him tell Jack how well he was doing and how good his life was upset me. I tried to talk to him on his own, but he always made sure that he came home when Jack wasn't away so there was no opportunity for this. Every time he left, he took something with him. One time after he left, I noticed that two silver frames were gone. He knew how much these meant to me and he still took them to sell. Another time he took my gold watch – I had a very difficult time trying to come up with a story to tell Jack how I "lost" it. I was on the brink of telling Jack everything, but knew that if I did, he would probably have a big argument with Greg the next time he came home and that Greg would never come home again. The thought of never seeing my son again was awful.

'Greg hasn't been home now in almost a year, I've spoken briefly to him twice in that time and he sent me three cards. I don't know what to do the next time he comes home, I have to talk to him and tell him that he's breaking my heart. He knows that I love him and he knows that I would never tell on him. Maybe he doesn't know how much he is hurting me.

'People often say a mother would die for her children – I've been dying inside now for eight years.'

10

WENDY'S STORY

Wendy is eleven years old. It is almost a year since her parents separated and she lives with her mother and younger sister. For three years, Wendy suffered at the hands of her violent father. She still has nightmares and will not go to sleep until she herself checks that all the doors and windows are locked. She looks like any eleven-year-old, dressed in jeans and an oversized sweatshirt. It is only when Wendy talks that it is evident that she is not like any other child her age. The trauma of a violent childhood has left Wendy with emotional scars that will fade with time, but never go away. Wendy speaks with startling clarity, revealing a disturbing insight into how terrifying domestic violence in the home can be for a child.

When I finish talking to Wendy, she jumps up out of the chair and bounds upstairs to finish knitting a coat for her doll. Her zest for life makes me believe that Wendy is successfully learning to be a little girl without an enormous weight upon her tiny shoulders. This is Wendy's story.

'I used to hate it when Daddy hit Mammy and made her

cry. Sometimes her nose would bleed or her eye would go all purple. I had to telephone for an ambulance once because Mammy said that she was very sick and needed to go to hospital. Daddy went out after he hit Mammy and I was very frightened that mammy was going to die. The ambulance came and took her away and the gardaí brought my sister and me to stay with Auntie Josie. It was nice at Auntie Josie's, but I missed my Mammy and wanted to go home. Mammy was in hospital for a whole week and we went to see her on Saturday. I got a fright when I saw her – she didn't look like my mammy. My sister started crying and then so did I.

'Daddy hit me really hard one time when I told him to stop hitting Mammy because she was crying and he was hurting her. I wished I was a big man and strong enough to pull him off Mammy. My sister and me tried to pull him off Mammy but we were too small. Mammy always used to tell us to go upstairs when Daddy was hitting her. Sometimes we would go outside and sit on the stairs listening to Mammy getting hit. Daddy would always go out when he stopped hitting her and if he saw us on the stairs he would come up to us and smack us hard. We always used to try to get up the stairs when the shouting stopped because we knew that he would be coming out.

'Once when I couldn't run away fast enough, Daddy caught me. I got such a fright I did a wee in my knickers. I hoped that Daddy didn't see what I had done, but he did and hit me with his belt because I had wet my knickers. He made me take them off and give them to him, then he washed my face with them. When Mammy came back from the shops, I told her what Daddy did and she sat down and cried. I was sad that I made Mammy cry. When Mammy asked Daddy not to hit me again, there was a big fight. My sister and I ran into the sitting-room but Daddy came in after us and grabbed my arm really hard. He pulled me all the way back to the kitchen and told my sister to come with us. Mammy was sitting at the table and Daddy pushed me on to the floor and Ruth [her sister aged five] ran over to me and cuddled into me. Daddy shouted at me that he didn't like tell-tales and told me that because I told tales, he was going to hurt Mammy. He said that it was all my fault. Before he started hitting Mammy, he said that if me or my sister moved he would hit us too. He got Mammy by the hair and banged her face off the kitchen table. He did this for a long time. He stopped doing this and went over to the washing machine. He took my wet panties out and rubbed them in mammy's face. Even though her nose was bleeding she was very brave and didn't cry. Me and my sister did. Daddy was really angry this time and kept shouting that he was the boss in this house. He kept telling Mammy to cry and she was saying "Not in front of the girls." Daddy said that he was going out and when he passed us, he banged our heads together. It hurt a lot and my sister and me had a bump on our heads. Mammy put ice-cubes on the bump and that made them stop hurting. Mammy cuddled us and told us that things would get better soon.

'One day when Daddy came home from work he was very angry. My sister was asleep in bed and me and Mammy were watching television. When Mammy heard the front door slam, she said to me to go to bed because there was going to be trouble – we always knew when there was going to be trouble. I got up and was going upstairs when I heard something smashing in the kitchen. Mammy screamed and I ran back to the kitchen. The window was broken and there was stew all over the floor. Daddy was breaking all the plates on the floor. I was afraid that Daddy would cut Mammy with a plate so I went in and asked him not to smash up the kitchen again. Daddy was always wrecking the house. He threw a cup at me and told me to get back to bed. The cup nearly hit me and I wet my knickers again. I ran upstairs before Daddy saw what had happened and my sister was sitting on the bed crying. Really fast, I put on clean knickers and hid the wet ones under my bed. My sister and me got into my bed and we hugged each other. We could hear Daddy shouting and hoped that he would go out soon. When we heard the door bang we ran downstairs and into the kitchen. There was lots of broken glass and broken plates everywhere and Mammy had a cut on her arm. We helped Mammy to clean the mess up and then we went to bed.

'Sometimes I wished that I didn't have a Daddy. Then I wished that my Daddy was like my friends' daddies. When I went to my friend's house, her daddy would play with us. There was no shouting and her daddy would tell us jokes. Sometimes I didn't want to come home from her house.

'I didn't know why Daddy didn't love me. He was always shouting at me and always hitting me. Even after he made me cry he never said that he was sorry. I knew that if somebody did something that they didn't mean to do then you should say sorry. Mammy said that Daddy couldn't say sorry – she said that he was sick. I asked Mammy could we not get the doctor to make him better.

'My teacher was talking about people who hurt us and I wanted to tell her about Daddy but I couldn't because it was a secret. Mammy told me that she would make it all better, but not to tell anyone about what Daddy did to us at home because it would cause even more trouble. I wanted the gardaí to take Daddy away and put him in jail forever – then Mammy wouldn't cry any more and me and Ruth wouldn't be afraid any more. Every night I wished that when I woke up, Daddy would have disappeared.

'Mammy told Daddy once that she was going to run away and take me and Ruth with her. Daddy laughed and said that he would find us and kill us all when he did. Mammy was frightened too. Me and Ruth used to talk about what it would be like if Daddy wasn't here. We used to talk about all the things we could do. At Christmas we had to be really quiet opening the presents Santa left, because if we woke Daddy there would be trouble. One Christmas he smashed all our toys because we woke him up. We knew that as long as Daddy was asleep there would be no shouting. We tried to be very good but Daddy would still hit us.

'One night I woke up and heard Daddy shouting, I heard him say he wanted us out. Then there was a lot of banging and I was crying. Ruth came into my bed and we listened until it stopped – then we fell asleep. The next morning Mammy woke us up and told us that we were going to stay in Auntie Josie's for a while. Mammy packed some of our clothes and our toys into cases and we got a taxi to Auntie Josie's. Daddy came around to Auntie Josie's and banged on the door but Uncle Bob told him to go away or he would call the gardai. Mammy was crying. Uncle Bob hugged her and said it would be OK. Ruth and I didn't go to school for a while. Mammy said it was best for us not to until things were sorted out.

'We moved to a new house and Daddy didn't come with us. We are in a different school now because our other school it too far away. I miss my friends, but my new school is nice and I have new friends. Ruth likes the school as well. We haven't seen Daddy in a long time and Mammy says that he will never hurt us again. I'm still worried that he will come and get us and I always make sure at night that even if he did come, he couldn't get in. Mammy, Ruth and me aren't so frightened any more – it's nice now because there's no screaming and shouting and we don't get hit. I hope that Daddy never comes back again.'

After the family home had been sold, Mick (the father) went to England where he now resides. There has been no contact with him in a year, and Lisa (the mother) and he are legally separated.

11

Vanessa's Story

Vanessa has just celebrated her eighteenth birthday. She lives in a flat on the outskirts of Dublin and has a steady boyfriend. From the age of nine, she was sexually abused by a male relative and also by her mother's boyfriend. Her mother physically and mentally abused her for eight years. As a result of this abuse, Vanessa attempted suicide and spent a period of time in a children's home. This is her story.

'My parents split up and I was nine years old when my mother had a new boyfriend. She had been going out quite a lot, and one night when she came home there was somebody with her. We didn't get a chance to see who it was because we were told to go to bed. The next morning my sister and I were introduced to him. He was going to be our new dad. He moved in with us and a couple of days later, the abuse started.

'I was sitting watching a film on television with him when he put his hands on my breasts which were starting to grow. He also fondled my legs. From then on he abused me. If I performed well with him, he wouldn't make me do as much housework and I could go out to play. If I didn't perform well he would make my life hell. I called him Daddy. I joined a club and made new friends but I never told anybody what was going on at home because I was afraid of what would happen if I did. I asked him to stop. I told him that I wanted to be like all the other little girls. He stopped abusing me sexually for a couple of weeks, but during this time the mental abuse was awful. He would pick on me all the time and made me do two hours of housework every morning before I went to school. The club organised an outing and I wanted to go. When I asked him for the money he said that I wasn't going and stopped me from going to the club altogether. After this argument the sexual abuse started again, I hated going to bed.

'My real dad had arranged to come and see us one weekend. My sister and I waited for him to arrive all day but he never came. We were so upset we went to bed. A while later the doorbell rang and it was my dad. We were a bit annoyed with him for not coming when he said he would, but we were glad that he had shown up. Peter, our mother's boyfriend, said that we could not go out with our dad. I got very angry when he said this and shouted at him that he wasn't my dad and he couldn't tell me what to do. Eventually my dad left and I was crying. Peter said that he was going to leave because he didn't need this kind of thing. When he said this my mother came over to me and told me that if Peter left, she would kill me. I knew that she wasn't joking so I had to apologise to Peter and ask him to stay.

'Peter got me a puppy because I had been a "good girl". One day my puppy got sick and Peter said that he would bring her to the vet for me. Instead, he brought her to the river and put her head under the water. He kept bringing her head above the water just to hear her squelch. In the end he drowned her. I was really upset about this because I loved my puppy.

'I knew my mother realised what he was doing to me. A couple of months after he had drowned my dog, around Christmas, Peter got drunk. He said that he had to leave because he did not want to be accused of anything that he had not done. Later on my mother asked us had he done anything. When we told her that he had, she got rid of him. But then she started to abuse me as if what had happened had been my fault. She kept punching me and asking me if Peter had ever told me that he loved me. This went on and on. My mother was pregnant at the time.

'I had very few friends and began going out with my sister. She was only a year younger than me and I made friends with her friends and met a boy. When my mother found out about this boy, she battered me. She dragged me around the room by the hair and when I fell on the floor, she kicked me until she was too tired to kick me anymore. During the next few months she would batter me around the place for no reason. She would punch, kick and bite me. I think that she was jealous of me because Peter wanted me. I don't know why she felt this way. I could never understand it. It was around this time she told my sister and me that we had all been invited to dinner. When we asked who had invited us, she told us that it was Peter. I couldn't believe that she was doing this to us. She wanted me to act as if nothing had ever happened. I told her that I didn't want to go but it didn't make any difference. We went to dinner. After we had finished eating dinner, my mother went to the shop to buy something for dessert. The minute she walked out the door, Peter was all over me.

'We had to stay at his flat every weekend. It was awful. We were not allowed into the flat during the day so my sister and I used to sit on the pavement outside. A woman used to give us biscuits to eat. The only time we were allowed to go into the flat, was when it was time for bed. Peter would abuse me sexually every time we were there. Soon me ma started seeing less and less of Peter and we didn't go over to his flat much now. He came over to our house to decorate it, I think it was only because of the baby that he did this. Soon after this, we found out that Peter had another girlfriend. All I can remember is that suddenly Peter was gone. Me ma was still pregnant. When she went in to have the baby I stayed with my granny. She took me in to see my mother and when we arrived at the hospital she was in the labour ward. After twenty minutes my mother had a baby girl. I was so glad that the baby was a girl because my mother told me before the baby was born that if it was a girl I could name her.

'I had turned twelve and it was coming up to the time when I was making my confirmation. I had been to the hairdressers to get my hair done and coming out of the hairdressers I bumped into the boy my mother had stopped me seeing ages before. We talked for a while and I arranged to meet him. We started going out together and one evening about seven, my mother saw us together. She was really annoyed and from that moment on, the baby, who was five months old, became my baby. My mother made me get up every morning to feed the baby and do the housework before I went to school. I lost a peg off the rain cover for the pram and she made me go out and look for it for two hours. I looked everywhere but couldn't find it and when I came home she battered me badly. I used to get beaten for every little thing. She would beat me for not making the bottles properly, for not dressing the baby properly, sometimes for no reason at all.

'When the baby was eleven moths old she started calling me 'Mama'. My mother went mad when she did this and began to take a little more interest in the baby. I was looking after the baby the day she took her first steps, I was so excited I spent the day trying to teach her how to walk. I was telling everyone what had happened but when my mother got in she told me to shut up. All during the school holidays I had to mind the baby, all day every day. It was as if she was my baby, I had to feed her, changed her and look after her. Sometimes a neighbour would take the baby just to give me a break, I think she felt sorry for me. I was so tired all the time, I had no chance to go out and play because I was in looking after the baby.

'I was in second year at secondary school when I met my first real boyfriend. He was the first person I ever told about what had happened to me with Peter and about what my mother was like. I had to tell him because I was always worrying. I was going out with him for seven months before ma found out. I was still getting beaten and had tried to find the right moment to tell her about Adam, my boyfriend, but there was never a right moment. Finally, one night she was in a very good humour and I decided to tell her about Adam; he was waiting for me outside the house. She asked me when could she meet him and I said right now! She liked Adam and actually approved of me seeing him. Everything was great for a while. I had been an A student in first year, and my mother thrived on all the praise she got because of this. She used to boast to people that it was because of her that my grades were so high. I didn't mind her telling lies; once she was happy she wouldn't batter me. However, I was seeing too much of Adam and my grades were falling. The fact that money was very tight didn't help the situation. I was in the house when my sister came in one night and said that she had been offered a job as a lounge girl, but she wasn't going to take it because it meant that she would have to wear a skirt. As soon as I heard this, I ran upstairs and put on a skirt. I went down to the pub and got the job, I would get £21 per week. I used to give ma £11 and keep £10 for myself. It was then that Adam began to beat me around the place, so I ended the relationship. I wondered what was wrong with me and why everyone beat me up.

'A couple of months after I finished with Adam, a customer in the pub asked me out for a drink and I told him that I was too young to drink. Then he asked me if I would like to go to the pictures with him, as his birthday was coming up. I decided that I would – the fact he was twenty-five didn't matter. He was great, a really great friend. I could talk to him about anything and everything and I did. He supported me. Just before Christmas, my sister started hanging around with the wrong crowd. She was getting into a lot of trouble and the gardai brought her home a few times. My mother was really annoyed about this, but her way of being annoyed was to lash out at my sister and me constantly. It got to the point that I did not want to come home after school. Although I wasn't doing well in school, I enjoyed getting out of the house and having fun at school. At school I could forget about everything at home.

'One night I was at work until about one in the morning and I came home very tired. My mother was out with one of her new boyfriends and my sister was out with her mates. The baby was in my aunt's. I left a note for my mother telling her that I would do all the cleaning before I went to school, I tidied the sitting-room and kitchen before I went to bed. It must have been about three o'clock when my mother got in. My sister still wasn't home. My mother came up to my room and started throwing the furniture around. She kept screaming at me and asking me where my sister was. She didn't give me a chance to answer and kept hitting me. She was dragging me around the room by my hair when my sister walked in. My sister grabbed my mother by the throat and warned her not to hit either of us ever again.

'My mother used to beat me with a big thick black belt about three or four inches wide. It had a huge buckle on it. This belt was one of the worst things I was beaten with, it hurt a lot and the pain would last for a long time. It was all horrible, a nightmare that just kept getting worse. One night before she has a chance to hit me with the belt, a neighbour stopped her and locked me in my room so she wouldn't get me.

'Things were going well for John and me. For once I

had a true friend, somebody I could trust. John used to collect me from work and make sure that I got home safely. One night my mother was out and John called to the house. My uncle was there and he and John got on really well. Unexpectedly my mother came home so my uncle told her that John was a friend of his. My mother accepted this story and talked to John for the rest of the night. The following day I told her that I was going out with John, but I lied about his age. When she found out how old he really was, she wouldn't let me see him any more. We still met, my mother was still bashing me a lot and John was always there for me. It was Valentine's Day and I called around to John's house. His sister told me that he had gone to buy me a card and flowers. I didn't see him all day and went to work that night. At the time John usually came in to see me there was no sign of him. It was at closing time that all the customers started to clap and cheer. When I turned around to see what was happening I saw John standing there with a big card and a basket of roses. They were so beautiful. John kissed me and told me that he would see me later. I was so happy I started crying. John never arrived to collect me so I went around to his house. His sister told me that he hadn't been home and that he was out with his brother. While I was on my way home, my mother was out looking for me. She had gone to John's house and started a fight with his sister. My mother had hit John's sister and pulled her hair. His sister didn't know what to do. When she got home she battered me. She kicked me, bit me, punched me and broke my nose. She did this in front of neighbours who were standing in our hall. I was in an awful state when I went around to John's house the next day, but he wouldn't speak to me and was very cold towards me. I went home and cried for hours. My mother had turned my only friend in the world against me. The next night I was at work when John came in and gave me a letter. It said that he was so sorry for being so cold. We started seeing each other again, I was so happy and so much in love. I felt I had somebody on my side.

'Some weeks later I was working. There was a big match on and the pub was really busy. John came in and bought some beer. He was going to watch the world cup match with friends somewhere else. Before he left, he came over to me and gave me a kiss. He said that he would be back later on to collect me. He never turned up so I went straight home. The next morning some of my school friends called as I was getting ready to go around to see John. When I answered the door to them, they asked me if I was all right. John had been killed in a hit-and-run accident the night before. I was lost. In that instant my world collapsed.

'Two years later, after an overdose and time in a children's home, I got my own flat and went back to school and did my Leaving Certificate I was seventeen years old.

'Some children need help in this country and Childline is not enough. Children need someone they can trust to care for them. This some parents just cannot do. I would like to say that I have forgiven my mother and that I do love her a lot. However, I do know that I would not be safe living at home with her. God will take care of my mother's ex-boyfriend and the uncle who abused me. I want to try and put the past behind me now.'

Since this interview with Vanessa, her mother's ex-boyfriend has been charged on several counts of sexual abuse and a court case is pending. Vanessa and her sister have both given statements to the gardai.

12

BILLY'S STORY

Billy is in his late thirties, separated and has no children. He has three brothers, all of whom are married, and his parents are both still alive. No one knows the hell he has been through during the past five years – it is a secret he says, he will take to the grave. He speaks out, in the hope that other men in his situation, will know that they are not alone. Billy is the person many people joke about – he is a battered husband.

'I suppose I'd consider myself to be a pretty normal kind of bloke. I enjoy a night out with the lads, I play a bit of squash, I smoke and I have a steady job. Most blokes my age have kids, I don't have any kids because Sue [his wife] didn't want kids. I'd love to have kids. I always thought I would have at least three. That was just one of my dreams she destroyed. I had it all worked out when I was in my twenties – I'd get married, buy a house, have kids and live happily ever after. What a joke.

'I was twenty-six when I first met Sue. It was about a year and a half before we started going out together. It took that long because Sue said that she wasn't ready for a commitment. I spent that year and a half asking her out and being refused. When she did agree to go out with me I was over the moon. Things were going grand and we decided to get married. We were both very happy and I had no idea of the life that lay ahead of me. Looking back now, I can see that we generally did what she wanted to do and went to the places she wanted to go to. I went along with her because if she didn't get her own way she'd sulk and rather than have her in bad humour, I'd give in. I've always been a bit of a pacifist, Sue called me a pathetic little man when we argued after we got married.

'The rows only started after we were married. I suppose that was because we both lived at home before the wedding and didn't spend twenty-four hours a day together. I can put my hand on my heart now and say that if I had known then what I know now, I would never have got married, not in a million years. I'm actually getting a bit embarrassed talking to you about it. I can't believe that this could ever have happened to me. I am an ex-rugby-player, for God's sake – I'm not exactly a seven-stone weakling. What that woman did to me, no one will ever know in full. I was so desperate once, I ran away. It sounds funny – at thirty-three years of age I ran away from home. I stayed away for only three days, I went back because I still loved her and hoped she would change. She managed to turn my love to fear and took away all the things I believed in. Don't get me wrong, I'm no wimp. The only thing that stopped me from hitting her was that she was a woman. I have been in fights with men, but I'd never hit a woman.

'After we were married we both worked and spent the weekends doing up the house. Sue decided exactly how she wanted the house decorated and insisted it should be done as quickly as possible. One day about two months after we were married, we had spent the whole day wall-papering. It must have been about 9 pm and I felt that if I didn't stop my arms would fall off. I asked Sue if she would like to go for a drink and she said that we weren't stopping until it was finished. I said to her that I was so tired I couldn't do any more. I began to climb down the ladder. She got into a temper. She said that she wanted the room finished because her parents were visiting the next day. I assured her that I would get up early in the morning and finish it before her parents arrived. She started screaming and shouting and saying that it had to be done right then. I continued getting off the ladder and before I had a chance to reach the ground, she threw a tin of paint at me. This might sound funny, but the tin of paint was full and the force of it broke my nose. I was so shocked that she did this but she didn't even bat an eyelid. The only thing she said was, "Now look, there's blood everywhere."

'Soon after we married, it got to the stage where I had to ask her before I accepted any invitation or made any arrangement to go out with my friends. It wasn't that she said I couldn't; it was just that she'd make my life hell if I did. Over the years the slagging from the lads changed from my being a newly-wed not wanting to leave the missus, to being a henpecked husband. It became a joke in work that if somebody wanted me to go out they should ask Sue first. I made excuses for her and for myself, I mean, no one wants to admit being afraid of their wife, do they?

'After about two years of marriage, I told Sue that things weren't going well. I told her that I didn't like what she was doing and that she must make an effort to change. The only response she made to my suggestion was to walk out of the room. It got to the stage where I would look forward to her going out with her friends. Before she'd go out though, she would leave me a list of all the things she wanted me to do while she was gone.

'She knew that I worried about money, I hated the idea of being in debt. She ran up massive credit card bills and handed them to me when they arrived. Our wages were paid into the bank. Actually the bank account was in her name. I had no access to this. Sue said that it made sense to have the account in her name because she looked after all the bills. God, I can't believe I was so stupid. Looking back now, I can see how pathetic I really was. I would do anything to keep the peace. I hated to argue. I actually used to jump when I heard her key in the door and make sure that I wasn't sitting down when she came in. Sue was very clever and made sure she had her loving moments with me. She'd tell me that she was sorry and promise to change. I suppose this is why I put up with it for so long. When she was loving she was like the woman I fell in love with and all the bad moments just faded away.

'As the years passed, the love I had for Sue lessened. So did the number of tender moments. I bent over backwards to please her but nothing I did was ever enough. I still have a scar on my arm from the time she threw hot oil over me. I was cooking chips for my tea one night and made a bit of a mess on the cooker. I had intended to clean it up when I had finished eating. I knew that there would be a row if I didn't. Anyway, I had just sat down to eat when Sue walked in. She saw the state of the cooker and started screaming that she wasn't going to clean it up. Then she got the chip pan and threw it at me. Luckily I had a thick jumper on, but the sleeves were rolled up and the oil burned my arm quite badly. I had to go to hospital to have it treated.

'I often thought about leaving but didn't want to lose everything. I knew that she could convince everyone that I was at fault and that nobody would believe me if I told what she was really like. It seemed the best thing to do was to stay. She was getting worse as time passed and I was at my wits' end. I told her that I wanted a separation and she replied that I would only have one over her dead body. She was very concerned about her image and it wouldn't do for her husband to leave.

'I was too ashamed to tell anyone. I didn't think that anyone would believe me, I think this even now. The end came when she had an affair. I knew that she was up to something. She was coming home late from work and going out at the weekends. It was as if she had a new zest for life. She would even be nice to me on the nights she was going out. I saw this as my chance to escape, but I didn't know how to approach her. I knew that she would cause trouble and I was afraid of the rage she might get into.

'I had a few drinks one night and waited for her to come home. I was feeling brave and determined to challenge her. When she got in I asked her where had she been, expecting her to give me a story. Instead she calmly told me that she had been out with her lover and that he was more of a man that I could ever be. She began taunting me and laughing in my face. For the first time in my life, I wanted to hit her. I wanted to punch her so hard that I would knock her out. Instead I left the room and went upstairs. Walking up the stairs I decided that I would go to a hotel and stay there until I could figure out what to do. The bank account was in my name now because she had run up huge debts and I was trying to get clear again. She still had her own account but she had transferred the household account to me because she didn't want the hassle and knew that I would take care of it.

'Anyway, she followed me upstairs and began taunting me again. She said that I wasn't a man and that she now had a real man. She started telling me about all the things she had done with her lover and said that she didn't love me any longer. I asked her what was she going to do and she said just continue as she had been doing. For the first time I shouted at her really loudly and told her that things couldn't go on like this. She picked up a brass clock from the dresser and threw it at me. I went to the hospital and got six stitches – she split my eye. She came to the hospital with me, not because she was sorry, but because she was afraid that I would tell what really happened and she'd get into trouble.

'When we got home, she had calmed down and said that we needed to talk. She said that she wanted the house, the car and the contents and she would agreed to a separation. It was too much. Even though I wanted to leave her, I couldn't let her have all this. I would be left with nothing. I said that I would agree to sell the house and split the proceeds, I said that she could keep everything that was in it and she could have the car. Sue agreed to this on one condition – that we told people that the reason for our separation was because I was having an affair. I agreed to this immediately as I was past the stage of caring. If it meant that I would be free of my living hell I would say anything. She wanted everyone to think that I was the big bad wolf and that she the innocent victim. I went along with this because I didn't want anyone to know the truth.

'The house was sold and the proceeds divided between us. She is living with another man now and my maintenance payments to her have ceased. Me? I bought a small apartment and live there on my own. I am still in the same job and the lads are trying to get me back in the land of the living again. I make excuses not to go out. I don't know if I'll ever be ready for another relationship again. My trust was shattered and because I was a man, I had nowhere to turn. People think that being a battered husband is just a figure of speech. It's not. I went through five years of hell and it will be a long, long time before I even think about trusting a woman again.'

13

NIALL'S STORY

Niall, who is in his early forties, is in the process of obtaining a judicial separation. He has two children aged twenty and fifteen. The fifteen-year-old lives with Niall. It is now almost five months since Niall left his wife of twenty-one years and he left because he simply couldn't take any more. Niall, who is an engineer by profession, is a victim of mental and physical violence in the home. This is his story.

'I was eighteen and she was seventeen when we first met. We got engaged a year and a half later, and married when I was twenty-one and she was twenty. Our daughter was born a year later. The first ten years were great – we had no problems. In fact the happiest times were when the kids were small.

'When we first married we had saved the deposit for a house but we decided to move in with an uncle and spend the money on his house instead. He was an alcoholic, but made us a promise that if we moved in he would give up drinking. This lasted nine months and then he started drinking again so we moved out and rented a house. We moved eight times in five years until we finally got a council house when our son was born. Our daughter was five years old then. When my wife came out of hospital after our son was born we moved in and we lived there for five years until we bought our own house. I was made redundant two years after this and things started to go wrong then. I got over £15,000 when I was made redundant, but this was gone in a year. The bank account was in joint names but I never took any money out. I'm not saying I didn't benefit at all from this money, but my wife did spend a lot more than me. She had a big chip on her shoulder about being as good as anyone, and she spent a lot of money getting her hair done every week to impress people and to show them she had class. A week after being made redundant I got another job, so there was never a time when money wasn't coming into the house.

'There were arguments and rows all the time now, mainly over going out and where we went. I was involved in sport, but she had no interest in this and didn't want to come with me. I gave it all up in the end – it just wasn't worth the hassle.

'My wife never got on very well with her own family and resented my being so close to my family. Her father grew up in a home and I think that his behaviour and hatred of authority rubbed off on her. The arguments went on for the next few years. Her father and mother moved into our house, her father caused havoc in the house. We had more rows about him than anything else. My wife resented the fact that her father never gave her any money towards anything. She would tell me to demand money from her father but I stayed out of it all and only spoke to the father when he spoke to me. My wife was never, ever left without money and we still went out at least twice a week, I always paid.

'My daughter was always a reserved child. She thought that her mother didn't love her and only loved our son. When she was seventeen, she left home because of the rows – she wanted to escape. She stayed with my mother for about six months. She came back home for three months and then left for good and got a flat. She is going to Al-Anon and other support groups and has be diagnosed to be suffering from severe anxiety. I've only realised in the past few months how traumatic it all was for her and how much she suffered as a result of her home life.

'We almost split up two and a half years ago when my wife was really drinking heavily. She left for a week and went to stay with her brother. During this week she went on a binge in his house. My daughter begged me to change the locks and lock her out of the house and my wife's brother wanted me to have her committed. I wouldn't do this to her and she came back. We went to see a psychiatrist in town and he told my wife that she needed help. A week later she cut back on her drinking and things seemed to be OK for about six months. She got a job and her drinking got worse. Then she picked up with this man whom she used to go out with two afternoons a week. It was about a year before I knew about this and when I asked her, she told me that they were just friends. I believed this and still want to but I was annoyed that she went out and left my son to come home from school to an empty house. We talked about this and she said that she would see him only once a month. I agreed to this, I knew that the only reason she was with him was for his money and because he bought her drink. That man has since been admitted to dry out. He says that if he ever sees her again he will kill her.

'As time passed, she was drinking very heavily again and began to get violent. Prior to this she wasn't physically violent as a rule. She would hit me across the face, knowing that I would not hit her back. She kept this up for months, but I never, ever hit her back. All I would say to her was: "Do it again if it makes you feel better." Of course this would make her worse.

'She began reenacting films. Her whole character changed; it was as if she was someone else. When her mother died from Alzheimer's disease my wife really went haywire. The night before her mother's funeral she went to a disco. On St Patrick's Day, we went out separately. We had been sleeping apart for about a month before this. When I got in that night she attacked me. Her friend was there and she tried to stop her, but she couldn't. My wife attacked me first with her fists, then with a brush and then with an iron. Her father and her friend saw this. I restrained her and told her that I wasn't going to let her go until she calmed down. She said that she was going to call the gardai, which she did. When they arrived, she told them to arrest me on the pretext that I had been beating her up. Her father told them what really happened and they were concerned for my wellbeing. The gardai advised me to leave the house, but I stayed because she had gone to bed and fallen asleep. The next morning she got up, wrote a cheque for £300 from my cheque book and vanished for three days. Her family wanted me to get her committed because they knew that she had a very big problem. When she vanished, I reported her as a missing person to the gardai.

'Three nights later we found out where she was, and her brother and his wife went to talk to her – she was staying in an hotel. When they returned after speaking to her, they told me that I would have to commit her because she was very unstable. In my heart I didn't want to do this. I went with them to the gardai to inform them that we had found her. The gardai arranged for a local doctor to go to the hotel and check her out.

'At this stage, I went to the hotel with her brother, the gardai and the doctor. She didn't know that we were coming and when we got to the hotel I couldn't face going in. I felt in my heart and soul that this wasn't right and I was half-hoping that they would come out without her. The doctor said that he couldn't find her insane and the gardai said that they couldn't believe how calm she was. She stayed in the hotel that night and I went home. She rang me a few times during the night and we had long conversations about what had happened and where we went wrong. I even agreed to see a psychiatrist with her just to get her to attend. Even at this stage, I was prepared to work at it. There was no talk of a break-up really. The next day, I was feeling very run-down and wanted to see my own doctor. During the night my wife had told me that our doctor had made an appointment for her to see a psychiatrist. I made an appointment and before I went I was talking to her on the phone. She was trying to dissuade me from going to the doctor. She actually rang me and asked me to collect her from the hotel at the same time as my appointment. I cancelled my appointment and made one for the next day, then I went to collect her. When I got to the hotel all she did was verbally abuse me. When I said that she had asked me to come and bring her home, she screamed that *she* would decide when she was coming home. I didn't know about the £300 cheque at this time and I wondered who was paying for everything. I left the hotel and went home. Shortly after I got home there was a phone call from her cousin, to say that she was bringing my wife home. Apparently this had been arranged well in advance and long before my wife asked me to collect her.

'Things were OK for the early part of the night. She went to bed but after about an hour she called me. She said that she had pains in her chest. I called the doctor, who came and gave her a sedative, and she went to sleep. She was to go for an X-ray the next day. The next day she applied for a barring order. When she got home she told me that she had done this to frighten me. She frightened me to death anyway. The gardai had advised me to take a barring order out some time before, but I didn't because I knew that she would take one out against me. The next day she tried to stop the barring order but couldn't. I went to the doctor the same day and found out that he had not made an appointment for my wife to attend a psychiatrist. Coming out of the doctor's, I met my daughter. She had seen my van parked outside and cornered me. She asked me to go and see a solicitor. She said that if I didn't, she would disown me. Even at this state I didn't feel that it was really over. I left my daughter and went straight into town to see a solicitor, I didn't have an appointment and hoped I would be able to see someone. My main objective at this stage was to get legal advice about a barring order. When I saw the solicitor, I asked him if I could stop legal action towards a separation, once I had started it. He said that I could. The solicitor advised me to lock my wife out of the house by changing the locks, I told him that I couldn't do this. We just talked about what a separation would entail and I left his office not knowing what to do. This was Tuesday.

'When I got home that day, my wife went on about how she was going to travel the world and get a mansion. The man she had been seeing was mentioned as her suitor. I believe she was friendly with him only for his money and the fact he bought her drink. For the next three days this was all she talked about. I told her that I had been to see a solicitor, so she also employed one. On Friday, three days after I had first seen my solicitor, he received a letter from my wife's solicitor demanding that I pay her £200 per week maintenance and all of the bills. My solicitor told me to give her nothing. She rang me on my mobile that day looking for her wages and I told her that she was getting nothing. She threatened to get the gardai up to the house – she had a protection order because she had applied for a barring order. I didn't know whether or not to go home, so I went to the gardai and asked them what a protection order was. They explained to me that she had the power to get me out of the house even if I had done nothing wrong. The gardai were aware of my situation and of her conduct. They offered to come to the house with me while I got my things. I told them that there was no need for this because she was out with a friend. When I got home, my son said that he wanted to come with me. We packed a few things and went to my mother's. My mother knew the situation and said we could stay with her for ever if we wanted to.

'About a week later, I got a call from the hospital at my mother's. A nurse informed me that my wife had been admitted with severe stomach cramps. I went to the hospital and she asked me to go to the house and get some things for her. When I got to the house, I asked a neighbour to come in with me while I got the things. The neighbour told me that the gardai had been at the house that morning and had actually brought my wife to hospital. I went back into the hospital and gave my wife her things. I made no reference to what the neighbour had told me. When I left hospital I went straight to the garda station to find out what she had done. The gardai told me that she had gone to the station that morning and told them that her father had poisoned her mother and killed her. The gardai came back to the house with her and took some bottles for testing. These bottles were clear and nothing more was done. The gardai knew what she was like.

'Over the next three days I visited her twice a day in hospital and we talked amicably about the separation. On the third day the doctors could still find nothing wrong and wanted her to see a psychiatrist. My daughter told her that they wanted her to see a psychiatrist and my wife assumed that I was going to try and have her committed again. The ironic thing is, I never spoke to a doctor or nurse, I didn't even know about this. When my daughter told my wife, they ordered a taxi and went off, leaving all my wife's things behind at the hospital. About an hour later, the hospital called my mother's asking was my wife there The gardai were also informed. Nobody could do anything. I went to collect my wife's things from the hospital and they told me that she was a very disturbed woman and needed psychiatric help, but there was nothing they could do unless she consented to it. My wife went home.

'The phone calls started the next day. She threatened to have me killed and my van blown up. One night she phoned me twenty times and then called her solicitor the next morning to say that I had phoned her twenty times. She was bringing teenagers to the house for drinking sessions. The gardai were called to the house twice for under-age drinking but no charges were brought. She was also going around with different men. My daughter told me that she was accusing me of tearing up her letter for the psychiatrist when I wasn't even in the house.

'About two months later I went to a disco with some friends. She came in all done up and asked me to go back to her. I refused and she asked me to leave her home. I refused again as I was afraid to be on my own with her. A couple of days later her friends rang me and told me that she had been crying all weekend and wanted me to go back because she still loved me. I told them that it was over between us and that I wasn't going back to her. The next day the parish priest rang me and asked me to meet her. I asked him was he aware of the situation and he replied that he was not, I explained to him that it was over and it was final. That was the last contact I had with her and that was two weeks ago.

'I feel so sorry for her. She's lost everything: her son, her daughter, her home and someone who deeply loved her. My son is much happier since leaving and is doing very well. He has told me that if I ever went back to her, he wouldn't come with me. My daughter and I are very close now, and I am now only beginning to realise how much all the trouble affected her. I know that with my help and the help of the support groups she is going to be fine. A part of me will always love my wife and I would like to see her getting herself sorted out. It may be too late for us, but it's not too late for her.

'If my story is part of a book that is written to help people, then I can let someone like me know that they are not alone. The worst thing is to think that nobody cares and you are alone. I'm lucky, I'm not. I have the support of a wonderful family and many friends behind me, which has made taking that first step so much easier.'

14

ADAM'S STORY

Adam is in his seventieth year, married for thirty-four years and has four children ranging in age from twenty-eight to thirty-three. He is currently on remand for breaching a barring order which has been in force since 1986. He believes that he has done nothing wrong and should not be in prison. This is his story.

'I was a sales rep during the early years and then later on started my own business as a painting contractor. I was very prosperous and bought a house in Drumcondra. All the trouble started when my eldest son was twelve years old. By the time he was eighteen he was battering me and continues to do this even now. My son was thieving and robbing cars and causing trouble at home. If I said anything to him, my wife would ring the gardai and say that I was the one causing trouble. She tried but failed to get a barring order through Free Legal Aid. I paid off the house and she has had the deeds in her possession for fourteen years. A while after being refused a barring brder, she employed a top Legal Aid lawyer to obtain an order and this time she was successful. On the 17 October 1986, I was barred on the grounds that I was causing trouble and drinking.

'Before she got the barring order, she assaulted me and I was injured. She split my head open with a sweeping brush and I was taken to hospital and had stitches in my head. I later discharged myself from the hospital.

'The year before I was barred, she fiddled £9,000 from my bank account. We were sitting by the fire one night and she asked me for money. I gave her ten pounds and told her that I would give her some more at the weekend. She was fiddling with the money in her hand and I told her to put it away. The next thing I knew the money was gone, she said that she had thrown it into the fire. I wrote her a note for the bank and gave her my bank book so that she could take £30 from the account. This account was in my name only. I now know the mistake I made was not to date the note of authorisation. Unknown to me, she continued to withdraw money until it was all gone. I had no reason to need the book and when I did ask her for it she would reply "Ah it's around somewhere." When I did go to the bank, I found out that there was only a couple of pence left in my account. Then I opened up a post office account. The following week, she took the money out of this account as well. I don't know how she managed to do this. I was very annoyed and argued with her because I had intended buying another house. She wouldn't talk to me about it. You couldn't talk to her; she wouldn't listen.

'I had a home, a car, a workshop and tools and when I was barred I lost all of these. She had the telephone number changed to ex-directory. She lied and said that I had been missing for years and got the telephone account put into her name. After I was barred, I moved into a bedsitter. I did a lot of work for the landlord, but when I had finished he wouldn't pay me. I stopped paying rent and he had me evicted. I got another bedsitter and worked on and off. I was in a bedsitter earlier this year and the landlord was a gangster. I paid my rent into his bank account, but because I was an old man he thought he could get me out so that he could let other people move into my flat. He got an eviction order against me and I appealed it. The date of the appeal was set for 23 March 1994 but on that date I was in prison for breach of the barring order. By a coincidence I was in court for breach of the barring order the same time as my appeal hearing. I got bail and I went over to the court where my appeal against the eviction had been heard. I explained why I wasn't there and I was given permission for another appeal. The date of the next appeal was 8 December 1994. I returned to my flat and a week later, the landlord brought the sheriff to evict me. It didn't matter that I had a date for a new hearing – he took no notice of this.

'All my belongings and possessions were taken out of my flat and put on to the street. People started coming over and taking my things. I was standing there watching them steal my things and I couldn't stop them. I just walked away, taking nothing. I went to my home and just stood outside it. I was arrested on the grounds that I was breaching the barring order because I was on the same road as the house. I was remanded in prison for a week before I got bail. I got out and I was on the move again. I booked into bed and breakfast accommodation most nights.

One night I tried to get accommodation but everywhere was full. I went to my home and sat on the pavement across from my house. I was arrested again and this time I received a six-month sentence. This sentence ended two weeks ago. When I got out of prison I looked for somewhere to stay. I went to the post office to get my pension book but it wasn't there. I went into town to the Department of Social Welfare and they said that they would do their best for me. They then gave me a letter for the Eastern Health Board so that I could get some money. I went to the Salvation Army to see if I could get a bed for the night there – there was no room. I then went to the Relieving Officer but the person I was dealing with was gone. I had been walking for hours and getting nowhere, so I decided to call to the home of someone who was in the St Vincent de Paul – they weren't at home.

'I decided to go to my last flat to check if there was any post for me. This route took me past my home. My eldest son was standing at the door and when he saw me he came over and knocked me onto the ground. He tore my jacket off me and held me on the ground with his foot for twenty minutes in the lashing rain. The gardai arrived and arrested me and I was taken to the station and charged with being drunk and breaching the barring order. Although I had a small bottle of rum in my pocket, I was not drunk. I had fifty pounds leaving the prison, and in my pocket I had the correct change after paying £4 for rum and £1 for a sandwich. I appeared in court and was remanded to prison. That is why I am here today.

'The house is in my name and has been paid for since 1976. I have a judicial separation and my wife won't sell the house. I've tried four different solicitors but no one will help. I have no contact with my children, who are all married. What can I do? I have no money and nowhere to go.'

15

JIMMY'S STORY

Jimmy is forty-four, has been married for sixteen years and has five sons. He is on remand at the moment for breach of a barring order. He has no previous convictions. It is evident from talking to him that he feels a huge injustice has been done and that he should not be in prison. He believes that he has done nothing wrong. His beliefs are typical of many men who have been imprisoned for the crime of violence in the home. This is his story.

'I don't think I'll get out tomorrow. I've been remanded twice. She appeared both times in court so I didn't get bail. She wants me to be locked up because she has a new relationship. That's the reason for the barring order. I realised that she had a drinking problem about six months ago. She's going downhill now. When I got out of prison seven months ago, I got a flat. She didn't visit me when I was in prison and it was about a month after I got out she got in touch with me. She wouldn't let me see the kids. I supported her and gave her money but then I stopped because the money was going on drink and not on the kids. We had a very happy marriage, I never once hit her even though she used to get a bit violent after drinking. She is a completely different person now. She's gone real hard – you know what I mean. I asked her to go for treatment three months ago, but she wouldn't. She told everyone lies. At the moment I am very worried about my kids. The eldest boy [fifteen] used to sit up worrying about his mam. She even got the phone cut off so I couldn't contact the kids. She won't let anyone come and see me and she will not talk to my family. My kids range in age from six to fifteen and I am worried about the younger ones being brainwashed by her and turning against me. If I can get over the next few weeks, then I'll know where I stand.

'She took the barring order out when I was in prison. We stayed in touch by phone; I've told you abut her getting in touch with me when I got out. Anyway, six weeks ago, friends of ours came to me and told me to speak to her because she was going around with men and going to hell. My eldest son used to work with me and when I asked him if this was true, he said no. At the weekend I would go around and wait outside the house, I would see her coming in at 3 in the morning. I approached her once and she called the gardai. I was taken to the station, but released the same night. I was in court two day's later, the judge gave out to me and I was released with a caution. Things got quiet. She sent a message that two of the kids were going on holiday and she asked for money. I had only just paid a big bill and I told her that I would send some money the following week. I went around when I got the money. I lifted the letterbox and shouted to her that I was there, then I put the money through the letterbox. The next thing I knew the gardai arrived and I was taken to the station, I was kept there overnight and I appeared in court the next morning. I was remanded in custody for a week and when I went back to the court the next week, I got out on my own bail of £500. I went back to work. She got word to me that if there was any work going for my son to let him know.

'A bit of work came up and at nine at night I drove to about half a mile away from where my wife lives. I asked a kid to go around to my house and tell my son that I had a bit of work lined up for him. After a while the kid came back and said that my son wasn't allowed around to see me. As the kid was talking to me, I saw a garda van drive by. I was arrested and that's why I'm in here now.

'I'm not a violent person and I feel that she has completely changed towards me. She's gone from being a very kind, loving person to a very hard person. I've spoken to counsellors about her seeing someone and getting help but they have told me that she has to go herself. If she had come clean with me months ago, then I wouldn't be in here today. I wouldn't have tried for a reconciliation if I had known there was someone else. I would just have got on with my life as best I could.

'She's getting deserted wives' allowance now. She also works in a crèche part-time and minds kids during the week. She must be bringing in over three hundred pounds a week, so why would she want me around. She'd lose all of that if I was there. I don't need social welfare, I have always looked after my family myself. The kids are not happy and are being brainwashed and there is not a damn thing I can do about it in here. I went to her father and asked him to try and help her, I told him about her drinking. He told me that he wasn't going to interfere. Even in here I have been talking to people and trying to sort things out. There has never been any violence and I have always provided for her and the kids. What more can I do?'

16

PAUL'S STORY

Paul is in his late thirties, married with two children, and lives in the south of Ireland. He has been attending counselling for the past year to help him come to terms with his violence. Drink was not a factor in Paul's violence. He had a very violent childhood; his father was physically abusive to him. Paul has been violent since childhood and admits he enjoyed being violent.

'I have always been violent even as a child. The results of my violence never had any impact on me, I always identified with violence as a way of obtaining things. My father was very violent – he was a real hard man. I was sixteen when I started hanging around with bouncers in city-centre nightclubs. I earned money this way and loved the power it gave me.

'I married at twenty-one and our first child was born shortly afterwards. My wife was still in college and we were living with her mother. I couldn't handle this child and got more violent. I would go into town and work for free because this gave me an opportunity to be violent; I got a great buzz from violence and I and the other bouncers used to compete to see which of us could be the most violent. It was like a sport to us, just like a game. Two of these bouncers are now in prison.

'Home and work were like two different worlds for me, but I was the gang leader in both. I had a good job with the health board, but I left this to start my own security business. I was doing between sixty and eighty hours a week and the pressure was awful. This got to me and I battered my wife continuously and didn't care. My wife learned to deal with things without involving me. I would come home from work and tell her that someone had battered me. She would just say "Ah well". The way I thought was; if I get hurt so what if she and the kid get a few knocks? My wife wasn't reared with this. I dragged her into this type of life. We were renting a house and I smashed it up. My two-year-old daughter stood there watching me. I never hid my violence from her. She witnessed it all. She is four now, but still remembers all the violence and my aggressive behaviour. Recently she said to me: "Remember the house that broke, Daddy?"

'The pressure of running my own business went on for about three years and all this time I battered my wife. Before I married I was never violent to any of my girl-friends. At the height of the pressure I heard a bloke talking on the radio about an organisation. He also talked about his own violence and how he was learning to overcome it. I contacted the group, but it was located in a place where I worked as a bouncer so I didn't go. I began to do raves and things were going downhill fast. We moved back to my mother-in-law's to live. I was considering giving it all up for about four or five months when I got injured one day and came home and went to bed. I stopped functioning. I was violent towards my wife and child, then aged two, all the time. I couldn't concentrate or handle the support people were trying to give me. I wanted to get help and my wife was very supportive.

'Two years ago, I started getting myself back to normal but I was still violent. Last year I had a very bad dream and when I awoke from it I battered my wife, who was asleep beside me. Two days later I attended my first meeting with the organisation. They explained things to me and I felt that I would now be able to get my life back together again. I had destroyed all close family relationships and I wanted to get back to normal again. A few months after going to meetings, my wife and I were in the kitchen. She was walking up and down and every so often she would look as if she wanted to say something to me but hesitated. It was a long time before she actually spoke to me. When she did, she told me that she had bought a new pair of trousers for me. I thanked her. Later that evening she told me that she was afraid to tell me because she was terrified of how I would react. Prior to attending the meetings, if she bought me anything I would give one of two responses. The first would be "Who are you to buy me trousers?" and the second would be "I'm not worth a pair of trousers." Either way there would have been trouble. A few weeks ago I got really, really angry with a battery; I was absolutely livid, it wouldn't fit properly into its holder. When I turned to tell my wife she was standing there laughing. I asked her was she frightened and she said no, I asked her was she still afraid when

I got angry and she said no. I think that I have made great progress. Having said that though, simple everyday things are still "situations" I have to deal with daily. If the kids are climbing on my front gate, I must psych myself up not to get annoyed. I constantly dream that I have slipped back into a violent life. That is something I hope never, ever, happens.'

17

JOHN'S STORY

John is in his late forties and lives in the west of Ireland. He has a very violent background and was sexually and emotionally abused as a child by his father. He is a reformed alcoholic and drug abuser and has been attending meetings to help him overcome violence for the past four years. He has also been a member of AA for the past twelve years. He has one son in his early twenties and is not currently in a relationship. Although he is reformed, he still admits to taking one day at a time. This is John's story.

'As a child I was abused and battered by my father. He used to make us all go to seven o'clock Mass every Sunday morning. My childhood was very violent and when my father died I challenged my mother about my early life. [John does not elaborate on this statement.] As I made the transition from boyhood to manhood, I carried the violence with me.'

[John lived a 'jetset' lifestyle, indulging his passion for violence and drugs. He took drugs and sold them. The friends he mixed with socially liked violence and derived a perverse pleasure from it. Orgies and hard drugs were part of life.] 'Part of me was saying "this is a great turn-on and part of me was saying, this is not what I want to do."

'I beat my son to a pulp one night – he was five years old. Shortly after battering him, I went up to him and asked him if he still loved me. I was constantly looking for love, but every time I gave my love I would take it back bit by bit because I thought it was being abused. I think my anger stemmed from the fact that I always tried to be a good person, but couldn't believe that I could actually *be* such a person. Before I left for work in the morning I would smash up the house. I couldn't understand when I came back from work that evening and nobody would talk to me. They just sat there shaking. As a batterer I didn't have the ability to trust another person. I needed to be in control all the time. My appetite for control meant that I found it necessary to degrade women. When I made love to my partner and climaxed, I would head-butt her in the face and tear her body to pieces. It took me eighteen months to overcome this after I sought help.

'I reared my son until he was sixteen; then he left home. I split up with my partner four years later and my son returned home. In the four years that he was away from home, we had a very unstable relationship and didn't communicate with each other very well. Now we have a good relationship. He has talked to me about the abuse and says that he forgives me. I can't forgive myself, though. He has a very mature attitude considering his youth.

'One Sunday I had been going around the house banging doors and smashing things. I grabbed my partner to batter her and my hand stopped in mid-air. I felt that at long last I had been cleared. The sense of power was overwhelming. My partner phoned the gardaí, but when they arrived I managed to convince them that my partner was mad. They left. For the next four hours I was on a high and so full of power, then I got depressed. My partner left, but before she did, she put a piece of paper on the phone with a number of an organisation to help men overcome violence. It took me five days to pick up the phone and call them. When I did, I felt that there was someone who really understood me. I felt that at last I could identify with other people. I went on a programme and attended meetings for a year. It was very tough and the programme made us analyse everything we did. I left after a year but found that I couldn't handle things, so I went back to the meetings. I learned that other people in my life were only giving me their "opinions" and that what they said was not gospel. One day there was an argument with my partner and I was trying to remain calm. I said to myself that my partner wasn't worth giving up all my hard work for. I was still verbally abusive, but this time I apologised afterwards. Shortly after this, my partner and I split up. The realisation of what I had put her and my son through dawned on me.

'It takes a long, long time for the shame to leave. I don't think it will ever leave me completely. It is a shame that every abuser carries. It's hard to describe how shame feels. When you begin to deal with your own violence, it's like switching on a television set and watching your life. The violence is there and there's no escape. I feel more secure in life now, but I still need the support of the meetings and I take one day at a time.'

Both Paul and John agree that seeking help was the best thing they ever did. They were taught that the little things they never even considered to be violent were in fact forms of power play. They were shown that withholding money from a partner is a type of violence. Very often the man would gain power and control by withholding money.

It is estimated that 70 per cent of married or cohabiting couples will at some stage experience some form of physical, mental or sexual abuse in the relationship.

Men sometimes find it relatively easy to stop being physically violent. However it is difficult for them to come to terms with verbal and psychological abuse and accept that these types of abuse are just as horrific.

The question most frequently asked is; 'Why doesn't she leave home?' The question that should be asked is; 'Why does he do it?'

18

CHILDREN
THE MOST INNOCENT VICTIMS OF ALL

Too often people assume that children are not aware of violence in the home and that it has no affect on them. In a small number of cases, there may be children who are not directly aware of violence directed at their mother. However, in the majority of cases children will witness violence against their mother – if not the actual abuse, then the effects of it (bruising, black eyes, tense atmosphere in the home). The children may well have been abused as well: almost 50 per cent of the men I interviewed who had admitted to battering their wives also admitted to battering their children. Many women seek barring orders only when they see the effect the violence is having on their children.

Every child will react differently to witnessing abuse. Some children will be deeply disturbed by such abuse, others will appear not to be disturbed and still others will react in ways so subtle that the root of the problem will not be obvious at all.

Abuse has psychological effects on children, the results

ranging from uncontrollable anger to utter helplessness. Many children will live in a state of terror for years. The consequences may include: anger, guilt, helplessness, stress, low self-esteem, insecurity, secrecy and shame, depression and lack of positive identity.

Often a teacher will be the person who notices that something is wrong with a child. Children's performance in school and their ability to learn can be severely affected. They may find it hard to concentrate and absorb new information because they are stressed and afraid and worried about the situation at home. The mother of a child I had spoken to told me that she had been called to the school by her son's teacher because her son had told him that his daddy was going to kill his mammy and he wanted to die before this happened. The boy was eleven. One woman said of her baby son: 'He was as near to a nervous breakdown as a fourteen-month-old baby could be.' Another said: 'He was screaming in fits when there was a row. Then he was torn between us. It was terrible for him to see so many glasses and doors broken. He's much better off now that we're away from him.' A lot of women spoke about their children's nerves being shattered and all noted a big improvement once the children were no longer subjected to violence, either if the mother took them to a refuge or the father or abuser was barred from the family home. All the children I spoke to said that they were glad that they had either left the father or that the father had left them. As one child said: 'It's great – we can talk out loud in the house now.' Another said: 'I'm not afraid any more and my mammy doesn't get beaten now.'

As discussed in the chapter on common myths below,

it is often perceived to be bad to take children out of their home even if it is to escape from constant violence. All the staff at the refuges agree – and after speaking to the children myself I too am of the opinion – that it is far more damaging for children to remain in a violent situation than for them to leave and go to the safety of a refuge with their mother. Also, in a refuge, both the child and his mother will have the opportunity to talk to others in a similar situation and realise that they are not alone. Some children will see their father through access arranged by the courts. Those attending school will continue to do so. If a child is in need of specialised help in the form of counselling or play therapy, refuge workers will assist the mother to making the referral to the appropriate agency or service. Refuges are only a stop-gap and ultimately the child will return to a family home with the mother.

Although it has been established that children do suffer greatly as a result of violence in the family home, they can be helped to overcome this trauma and its effects with love and support. Children are resilient and, for many, eradicating the problem by removing the abuser may be sufficient to ensure they grow up to be confident and secure adults with no lasting scars.

19

COMMON MYTHS

1 ALCOHOL CAUSES BATTERING

Alcohol does not make a man abuse his partner or child. Very often it is used as an excuse, but it is never the cause of habitual battering. Many victims of violence in the home have suffered at the hands of abusers who were sober at the time. It must also be taken into consideration that many men who do drink do not batter their partners and children. 'It was the drink that made me do it' is often the excuse given for violent behaviour.

2 WHY DOESN'T SHE JUST LEAVE HIM?

Any woman who has been a victim of violence in the home truly wishes it were as simple as that. Some women are simply 'too broken to fly'. Having been degraded by their partner for so long, they put no value on their self-worth. Constantly being told what to do and when to do it, with severe consequences if instructions are not precisely carried out, has a dire effect on the woman's state of mind. Abused women choose to remain in a violent situation for many reasons and many are financially dependent on the abusive partner. Those living with a partner who is violent only to them stay for the sake of the children – it is the children's home and they feel that it would be detrimental to their wellbeing to uproot them and remove them from their friends, school and only life they have ever known. Many worry about how they would manage if they left the security of the family home, both financially and emotionally. Many live in fear and know that if they did leave they would be found and probably beaten to death by their partner. Some believe that their marriage vows – for better or for worse – means that they must endure constant beatings. Many hope that the beatings will stop. Many think they have no one to turn to for support, many do not want the stigma of being a 'battered wife'. Most are brainwashed into believing that there is no option but to stay.

3 DOMESTIC VIOLENCE IS CONFINED TO THE WORKING CLASSES

The crime of violence in the home is not confined to any social class. There are battered women all over the world who have no vivid scars branding them 'battered wives' and nothing about their physical appearance gives any indication of the life they are forced to lead. The majority of middle- to upper-class women choose to remain in the family for the sake of the children and to avoid the stigma of being a 'battered wife'. Perhaps it is because those who avail of refuges tend to be working class, have no access to money and cannot pay for alternative accommodation. Helplines frequently receive calls for help from wives and partners of judges, doctors, teachers, politicians and businessmen. The majority are financially dependent. Physical, mental and sexual violence in the home pervades all social classes and no one aspect is more prevalent in any class.

4 SHE MUST ASK FOR IT

No woman I interviewed 'enjoyed' being abused. This assumption is perhaps the cruellest of all. No woman asks to have her nose broken or her jaw smashed. No woman asks to be beaten so badly that she miscarries her baby. No woman asks to be burnt with cigarettes or branded with a hot poker. No woman asks to be brutally raped, or to have her children scream in fear. With a violent man, provocation constitutes asking for money to feed the children, or asking what time they will be home. A woman's submission should never be confused with consent. No woman deserves to be beaten to a pulp under any circumstances.

5 MEN WHO ARE VIOLENT COME FROM ABUSIVE FAMILY BACKGROUNDS

This is not true of all violent men. Some men who are violent come from violent backgrounds; some men who come from violent backgrounds do not abuse. Many men who do not come from violent backgrounds abuse women. Sixty per cent or more of all married men are responsible for violence towards their wives in one form or another: add to this a similar proportion of men in non-marriage partnerships.

6 IT'S SELFISH TO TAKE THE CHILDREN
AWAY FROM THEIR HOME

'It got to the stage where my husband used to go up and beat the children with a stick while they were sleeping.'

'My three year-old tried to pull her father off me when he was beating me with his belt.'

'My six-year old son told his teacher that he was afraid that daddy was going to kill mummy.'

'My ten-year old son began beating his younger sister who was four. When I asked him why he did it, he told me that he was a man and he could hit women like daddy.'

'Every time my husband punched me, my daughter would bang her head off the wall. She became very withdrawn and began wetting the bed.'

'Once the kids heard his key in the door, they would stop what they were doing and run in to me.'

'My son took an overdose – he was nine years old.'

These are factual statements from battered women who knew that their children were being damaged by their abusive fathers. Many women leave home as a last resort after exhausting all other possibilities. Research has shown that children are more damaged by remaining in a violent situation than by leaving. The physical and emotional health of children actually improves once they have been removed from the situation.

7 IT'S NONE OF OUR BUSINESS

Domestic violence is a social problem and the abuse of another person is everyone's business. Many women are forced to stay in a violent situation because they believe that nobody cares. They are surprised when they ring a refuge or a helpline to find that there *are* people who care and understand. Many people listen to the screams of women and children being battered and do nothing for fear of being denounced as an interfering busybody. It is the reluctance to make that call that may result in a woman or a child sustaining horrific injuries. People should realise that victims often feel alone, afraid, ashamed and are living in fear. Many have been told that they will be killed if they divulge details. All victims need to know that there is somebody there that they can turn to for help. It is not very useful to say to a battered woman: 'Why don't you just leave?' It is never that simple. Try to understand this before appearing to be pompous or dogmatic about something you know very little about. Victims don't need lectures. Very often all they want is somebody to talk to, someone who will just sit there and listen without passing moral judgement.

8 IT DOESN'T HAPPEN

Twenty-five per cent of violent crime against women is inflicted in the home. In one four-month period, gardai received 1,658 calls for assistance in the Dublin Metropolitan District alone. These were only the reported cases – it has been estimated that there may be more than five times this number that are not reported. Domestic violence is the most silent crime and least reported crime of all, leaving in its wake victims who have been bruised, battered, maimed, tortured and sometimes killed, often without anyone knowing what has been happening until it is too late. 'The home is the most dangerous place in modern society. A person of any age or of either sex is far more likely to be the subject of physical attack in the home than on the street.' (Giddens, 1989)

20

STATISTICALLY SPEAKING

Incredible as it may seem, there are no official nationwide statistics in Ireland documenting the extent of violence in the home against women and children. This crime is particularly horrendous because many of its victim are too frightened to report it and their silence will never be broken.

IRELAND – AVAILABLE FIGURES

- In 1993, the Women's Aid National Helpline received over 6,000 calls. Between November 1991–1992, 529 women sought refuge at the refuge in Rathmines. It could accommodate only 149. The refuge deals with an average of ten emergency calls every day. (These are calls from women who fear for their lives and who need immediate refuge.)

- Between 1990 and 1993, Aoibhneas, situated on the northside of Dublin, accommodated 220 women and 367 children. At any one time, up to four families will share one of the two bedrooms. It has responded to over 3,000 calls for help and facilitated over 1,000 day visits to the refuge.

- In a four-month period in 1990, gardai received 1,658 calls for assistance in domestic violence cases in the Dublin Metropolitan District. In 1993, The Women and Child Garda Unit received over 5,000 calls for help due to 'domestic violence' situations in the Greater Dublin Area.

- According to the National Crime Survey data, 1973–1977, 95 per cent of assaults on spouses are committed by men. In addition, the extent of injuries sustained by men were found to be insignificant compared to those sustained by women. (Department of Justice, *Report to the Nation on Crime and Justice*).

- It must be noted, that the statistics quoted, with the exception of the National Crime Survey data and figures for calls to helplines relate only to the Greater Dublin Area.

21

Worldwide Statistics

USA

Battering is the single biggest cause of injury to women. Four thousand women yearly are beaten to death by their partner. (Koop US Surgeon General, 1989.)

Canada

Thirty-nine per cent of women reported having been sexually assaulted at some time. (Canadian National Survey, 1993). One in ten Canadian women will be abused or battered by her husband or partner. (*Wife Battering in Canada*, Canadian Advisory Council on the Status of Women, 1980.)

Sweden

One woman is battered to death every ten days. There are 115 refuges in Sweden and they are constantly full. (Rooks, 1990)

BRITAIN
Twenty-five per cent of women have been abused by their husband or partner. (Dobash & Dobash, 1979)

MEXICO
A woman is raped every nine minutes. (*Doble Jornada*, November 1987.)

THAILAND
In Bangkok, Thailand, 50 per cent of married women are regularly battered by their partners. (*Worldwatch Institute Report.*)

INDIA
An estimated 1,000 women are burned alive each year in the state of Gujarat, India, alone. (Ahmedabad Women's Action Group Report)

TANZANIA
Six out of ten women have experienced physical abuse from their partners. (*Violence against women in Dar-es-Salaam: a Case Study of Three Districts.* Tanzania Media Women's Association, 1989).

The Irish and worldwide statistics on violence against women demonstrate the appalling reality. 'The home is the most dangerous place in modern society. A person of any age or of either sex is far more likely to be the subject of physical attack in the home than on the street.' (Giddens, 1989)

22

THE LAW AND WHAT IT MEANS

Once a decision has been made by the victim to leave an abusive relationship and to instigate legal proceedings, inevitably there will be a consultation with a solicitor and a court appearance. From the moment the victim enters the often complex world of the 'legal system', he or she will face a barrage of legal jargon that is often hard to understand. It can also be difficult during this traumatic time to assess all the options available and decide which is best for you. This chapter lists the various options open to you, and terms that may be used by your solicitor and also in court. Prior to leaving an abusive relationship, it is advisable to report any physical assault or abuse to both your local gardai and your local doctor or hospital, even if you are not taking legal action at the time. Evidence of physical violence, including photographs of injuries, is vital for some of the legal options open to you.

Once you have decided to instigate legal proceedings, you can go by yourself to the District Family Court in your area, and apply to take out the following orders:

Protection Order

As there is usually a time lapse from the date an application for a barring order is made and the date of the court hearing, a protection order is normally granted immediately. However, a protection order will be granted only if an application for a barring order has been made.

A protection order permits the violent partner to continue living in the family home until the court hearing for the barring order takes place. The offending spouse (a protection order can only be taken out against spouses) is ordered not to use or threaten violence against the other spouse or children before the hearing for the barring order. Once a protection order has been taken out, the offending spouse will receive a letter in the post from the court telling him that an application for a barring order has been made, and gives the date of the hearing.

It is widely believed that a protection order is a totally inadequate measure and does not reassure the victim. Because the offending spouse is allowed to continue living in the family home, many women feel too frightened to remain there. This factor contributes greatly to women seeking safety in a refuge until the court hearing. Ninety per cent of women interviewed said that they do not feel safe with a protection order.

Barring Order

Many more women than men apply for a barring order. In a survey of 1,222 applications for district court barring orders, in only 25 cases was the husband seeking to bar the wife; in 11 cases the information was not available; and in 1,186 (97.9 per cent) of cases, the person seeking the barring order was the woman. (Peter Ward, *Irish Law Times,* 1988, 6).

The term 'barring order' is perhaps the most widely recognised term to the person on the street, but what does it really mean?

A barring order is an order that prevents the offending spouse from attending, residing in, or entering the family home for the duration of the order. One must go to the district family court to obtain such an order. It is not necessary for the spouse applying for the order to be living in the family home and the offending spouse does not have to be living in the family home to be barred from entering it.

Many people believe that anyone can take out a summons for a barring order; this is not the case. Taking out a summons for a barring order is restricted to a spouse. Unmarried women are unable to seek a barring order for an abusive partner (see Injunction), nor can a child take out a barring order against an abusive parent for instance in the case of sexual or physical abuse. (In this situation the onus to take out the order lies with the non-offending parent.) If a parent is being abused by an adult son or daughter, it is not possible to get a barring order to prevent them from entering the home; the only option available in this situation is to apply for an injunction (see below).

It is also widely believed that a barring order is effective immediately after a summons for one is issued, and again this is not the case. There is usually a period of waiting for a date for a court hearing. A copy of the protection order will be sent to the offending spouse at the same time as the barring order summons. A copy of this is also sent by the district court clerk to the local garda station.

The spouse seeking the barring order is required to give evidence in court in relation to the extent of violence, the injuries sustained and why they want this order. They should have a solicitor in court and also bring any witnesses who would be prepared to speak on their behalf. The evidence of doctors, social workers, family and friends is very important and sometimes crucial. It is up to the spouse seeking the order to bring any witnesses to the court.

Both spouses will attend on the date of the hearing. However, if the offending spouse does not turn up and no reason is given to the court for his absence, the hearing will continue and his absence will not prevent a barring order being granted. On the date of the hearing either spouse may ask for the hearing to be adjourned. After considering this request and the reasons given, the judge may or may not adjourn the case.

All applications for barring orders are heard in private: only the spouses, their legal representatives, witnesses, the court clerk and the district judge will be present. Although one can represent oneself in court, it is not a good idea to do so. A courtroom can be a very intimidating place and sometimes it can be difficult to understand what is being said and what is going on. It is also important to remember that the offending spouse will most likely have legal representation. For those living on a very low income, it is possible to apply for free legal aid (see section on FLA), or, alternatively, to employ the services of a solicitor (see Solicitor).

Once the hearing begins, the spouse applying for the

barring order will be asked to give evidence firstly regarding the reasons for the application. The offending spouse or his solicitor may then ask questions. Next, any witness supporting the application, including the family doctor, social worker, gardaí, family or friends, will give evidence. After this, the offending spouse (if present), will give evidence, and may then be cross-examined by the applicant for the order, or their legal representative. The judge may question either spouse at any time during the hearing. If the judge is satisfied that there is a risk to the safety and welfare of the applicant and/or the children, a barring order will be granted. A barring order is usually granted where there is a history of violent behaviour, including violence and verbal abuse, and/or the family is living in fear of repeated attacks.

If a the barring order is granted, the offending spouse may appeal to the circuit court to have the case heard again. An appeal must be made within fourteen days of the district court order.

The district court has only the power to bar the offending spouse for a period not exceeding twelve months. In order to have the barring order renewed, it is necessary to reapply after this period of time. An application for a barring order granted by the circuit court is usually for an indefinite period and may in some cases be permanent.

The district court order usually makes provision for preventing the offending spouse from threatening their spouse at his/her place of work, or from approaching him/her when the children are being collected from school or from following him/her or the children. The court will give custody of the children to the spouse who obtained the order, and will made some provision for the offending spouse to have access to them.

If the offending spouse breaks the order by coming to the house and trying to gain entry, or by harassing their partner or children, the gardai should be contacted at once. If the spouse is found in or at the family home they can be arrested and charged. Even if they have left the scene by the time the gardai arrive, the gardai have the power to arrest them if they are satisfied that the order has been broken. If an offending spouse breaches the order, in Dublin the case will be heard in a criminal court as opposed to a family court, and the offender will be liable for a fine of up to £200 and could also be committed to prison for a period of up to six months. In areas of smaller population, the same district judge who granted the barring order will probably hear the case.

In some cases, after a cooling-off period and perhaps long and frank conversations, the spouse who has been granted the barring order may decide that they now want the offending spouse to come back and live at home. They believe that the offending spouse is sorry and that it is now possible to make a fresh start. This scenario is quite common, but unless it is dealt with through the proper chanels, it is illegal to make arrangements like this. For a spouse to take an offending spouse back into the home whilst a barring order is in effect, the offending spouse is in fact committing an offence. If a couple have decided to reconcile and the offending spouse wants to return to the family home to live, it is necessary for them to apply to the district court to have the order discharged.

INJUNCTION

Since a protection order and a barring order can be taken out only against spouses, an injunction is the only resource available to people who are not married to their abuser, such as unmarried partners and abused parents. An application for an injunction is taken out in the local circuit court. It is necessary to have a solicitor acting on the behalf of the person seeking the injunction. An injunction orders a person to stay away from the abused and their home. If it is broken, the offending person can be taken to court and fined or imprisoned.

MAINTENANCE ORDER

A maintenance order can be taken out to obtain financial support for the abused spouse and dependent children. A spouse can apply to the court under the Family Law (Maintenance of Spouses and Children) Act, 1976, for an order making the offending spouse pay 'periodical sums' for the maintenance of the applicant spouse and for the children of the marriage. A maintenance order may be taken out at any time. There is no stipulation that the abused spouse has to be living apart from their abuser. In the situation where one spouse has a drink, drug or gambling addiction and is not providing enough money for the family to live on, the other spouse can apply for a maintenance order even though they are living and intending to continue living with their spouse.

An application for maintenance in the district court involves filling out a standard form which is called a summons. When this is taken out, a date will be given for the hearing. However, if the applicant is in need of maintenance before the date of the court hearing, it is possible to apply for an interim order. This order will be valid only until the case for maintenance is heard. The spouse against whom such an application is to be made must be informed. If they refuse to pay any maintenance and the applicant is unable to survive, the applicant may apply even before the case is listed for some maintenance pending the hearing of the case. This is quite rare, as the case is usually heard within a short time, normally six to eight weeks. During this time, the applicant can apply to their local health centre for supplementary welfare. The district court is restricted in the amount of maintenance it may award. The ceiling is up to £100 per week for the spouse and up to £30 per week for each dependent child.

When the case is heard in court, both spouses will be asked to give evidence and a statement of income. The applicant will have to show that, given the financial circumstances, their spouse has failed to provide adequate maintenance for them and the children. It is important to note that if the spouse against whom the order has been taken out is in receipt of social welfare payments and the applicant is interested only in getting money every week to survive, then it is possible to arrange separate social welfare payments at the local exchange. In this case it is not feasible to apply for a maintenance order.

When the district judge has considered the details of income and outgoings of the person against whom the maintenance order was issued, and is satisfied that adequate provision has not been made for the family, he/ she will then decide on the amount that they are liable to pay to their spouse on a weekly or monthly basis. Both spouses have the right to appeal from the district court to the circuit court, where the case will be heard again. Normally an appeal is made to the circuit court if the amount of maintenance awarded by the district court is not enough, or if the application for maintenance was refused by the district court. An appeal must be lodged to the circuit court within fourteen days of the district court order. Contact the circuit court office regarding this procedure.

If the applicant is satisfied with the outcome of the district court, their spouse will be ordered to pay the maintenance through the district court office. It is paid to the district court clerk, who in turn will send it to the applicant. If, however, the applicant is unhappy with this arrangement alternative arrangements, such as having the money paid directly into a bank or post office account, can be made.

Unlike the district court, there is no standard form on which to apply for a maintenance order from the circuit court. The applicant is permitted by the circuit court to use means to find out their spouse's earnings before the case is heard. There is no limit to the amount of maintenance the circuit court can award, and this, together with the fact that legal advice is needed to make an application, is the main difference between the circuit court and the district court. There is a right of appeal from the circuit court to the High Court, where the case will be heard again.

It is more complicated and difficult to apply for a maintenance order in the High Court than either the district or circuit courts. The High Court, under the 1976 Act, has the power to hear applications for maintenance orders but the vast majority of such applications are made initially in the district and circuit courts. The High Court can award any amount of maintenance to be paid, and as this is the highest court, there is no appeal; the decision of this court is final.

There are two options available to someone who has been awarded a maintenance order and whose spouse has failed to make the payments:

1   If the person against whom the order has been made is in paid employment, then it is possible for their spouse to apply for an *Attachment of Earnings Order*. A summons is issued to the offending party and they must appear in court. If the court finds them to be behind in their payments, it may rule that the amount of maintenance and a certain amount for arrears be deducted by their employer before any wages are paid. However, the court will ensure that the amount left after these deductions does not fall below the *Protected Earnings Rate*.

   The court has the power to enforce certain orders, one of which is an order requiring the employer of the person against whom the maintenance order has been taken out to give a statement of their employee's earnings to the court. An Attachment of Earnings Order is subject to change if, for example, the spouse changes job. An order may be ended at the courts discretion, on the application of either spouse. An Attachment of Earnings Order can only be used when the spouse is an employee.

2   The second option available in the case of default of payments is the issuing of a warrant for the arrest of

the defaulter. This may be done under the *Enforcement of Court Orders Act 1940*. This order means that the offending spouse is brought to court, and if the other spouse can prove that they have deliberately defaulted with payments, then they are liable for a prison sentence of up to three months. In addition to this, their goods may be sold and the proceeds used to clear the arrears. It is possible to recover up to six months arrears by this method. This order is rarely enforced by the court.

A survey has shown that of 636 district court maintenance orders in existence on 31 July 1986, only sixty were fully paid up, and in over 50 per cent of cases there were arrears outstanding for over six months. (Peter Ward, UCD, June 1989).

CUSTODY ORDER

It is possible to apply for a custody order at the same time as a barring order. This is taken out to gain custody of one's children. It is possible to take out an order for custody on one's own and free of charge, but it is advisable to have legal representation. Access to the children by the other parent is decided by the judge. Very rarely is access denied, one of the few reasons being for sexual abuse. In cases of suspected child abuse, supervised access may or may not be permitted. It is generally believed that it is important for children of separated parents to continue seeing the parent who does not have custody. Terms of a custody order are not final and further applications may be made to the court to have the order reversed or altered due to circumstances. A custody order is valid only for children up until the age of eighteen. The decision of the court must be adhered to by the custodial parent. Failure to comply renders the offender liable to a fine and/or a prison sentence.

23

LEGAL AID

Legal aid was introduced by the Irish government in 1980. Prior to this, Josephine Airey brought a case to the European Court of Human Rights because she could not afford to employ the services of a solicitor to represent her in her application for judicial separation from her husband.

The various voluntary organisations and refuges that care for victims of violence in the home are agreed that the legal aid system is totally inadequate. For example in Tallaght, which has an estimated population of 120,000 and rising, a person can expect to wait up to twelve months for legal aid. There are waiting lists at all of the legal aid centres, and the whole system is grossly under-funded by the government. The extent of this under-funding is especially visible when certain centres refuse to accept any new applications in an effort to deal with the backlog.

Legal aid was introduced to help people who were not financially in a position to pay for legal advice or represent-ation. The waiting list for legal advice is far shorter than for legal aid. Legal advice involves a consultation with a solicitor or barrister to discuss a given situation to find out what the best course of action is, and what options are available, whereas legal aid entails representation in court by a solicitor or a barrister. Legal aid is means tested, and generally those who are in receipt of social welfare as their only source of income would not have to pay anything for this service. Anyone wishing to find out about the eligibility conditions for legal aid should contact a legal aid centre. (See addresses at the back of this book.)

Once an application for legal aid has been accepted, (application forms are available at any of the law centres), and the applicant qualifies for legal aid, an appointment to see a solicitor will be made, though the applicant must be prepared for a long delay, especially in Dublin. However, although there are long waiting lists at all the centres around the country, the Legal Aid Board *does* have the power to grant emergency certificates. If the applicant or their children are in physical danger and fear for their safety, then this would be considered to be an emergency and a certificate would be issued immediately. These certificates are issued only in very urgent and extreme situations. There is a right to appeal any decision that has been made and one may contest eligibility. The appeal may be made to the Legal Aid Board.

FLAC

Free Legal Advice Centres, or FLAC as this system is more commonly known, is not part of, or affiliated with, Legal Aid. FLAC was set up to campaign for a comprehensive scheme of legal aid and advice. Even after legal aid was introduced in 1980, FLAC continued to campaign for *adequate* legal aid services. At its centres around the country, staff consisting of solicitors and barristers voluntarily give advice. FLAC does not represent people in family cases but volunteers do offer advice concerning legal rights, options and support groups. FLAC continues to campaign for adequate legal aid services.

The voice of the people is the loudest of all, and if the legal aid system is to be revised and adequately funded by the government it will only happen as a result of public outrage. Tackle your local TD, lobby outside the Dáil, campaign for what should be a fundamental right. It is time for the government to accept that the legal aid system is inadequate and the time for change is now.

24

WHAT THE PROFESSIONALS SAY

DR ART O'CONNOR, CONSULTANT FORENSIC PSYCHIATRIST,
CENTRAL MENTAL HOSPITAL

'There is a socio-economic difference: crime, drugs, alcohol and unemployment are all factors of working class. Education, or lack of it, also has some relevance; people who have had a poor education cannot articulate well and therefore would use violence instead of words. This type of violence is not as apparent in the middle and upper classes.

'I am a great believer that one is responsible for one's actions. It is wrong to attribute them to drink or drugs. Suddenly, we are to be guilty because of this. There are people in society who are nasty and difficult and who express themselves in terms of violence; these people are downright bad. The adult who batters is not someone with deep psychological problems; he batters to get his own way. He doesn't batter people in the pub because they would batter back. It's a wishy-washy but well-meaning notion that society is to blame. For whatever reason, these people are responsible for their actions. I cannot understand why people have the right to kill their wives/lovers because they are having an affair, a crime of passion. To be violent when one is jealous is deemed to be acceptable; this is wrong.

'Adults try to control children by hitting them. The only reason one is violent is because the victim is smaller.

'Professional people see these men and try to evaluate them and ascertain the cause of the problems: society, drink, drugs and so on. I have come to the conslusion, that there *are* in fact, *some* men who are naturally evil and bad.'

Tammy Berry, Social Care Worker

'My job entails working with emotionally disturbed children. On a regular basis, I work with children who are, or have been, subjected to violence in the home.

'Children often feel that they are to blame and that they have somehow caused this situation. Others feel protective of an abused parent or sibling, while in other cases, children see it as a way of life and model themselves on the behaviours exhibited. However children perceive the situation, it will have an effect on them, generally a damaging one.

'Some children become withdrawn and introvert, often regressing and exhibiting such problems as 'enuresis' (involuntary urination) or 'encorpresis' (holding back a bowel motion or soiling). Others may punish themselves out of blame – and seek control which is often found in food disorders such as anorexia or bulimia, whilst others copy the behaviour and become abusive or aggressive, which often leads to conduct disorders.

'It is of crucial importance to highlight the fact that such traumatic situations leave their scars on children which surface, either in childhood as explained above, or in later adult life when relationships are being formed.

'Therefore, regardless of how a child is affected, it is vital to be aware,that unless the problem is tackled and eradicated with professional help, it can lead to lasting emotional damage.'

JOHN LONERGAN, GOVERNOR, MOUNTJOY PRISON

In an effort to understand the behaviour of a perpetrator of violence in the home, I went to Mountjoy Prison and spoke to John Lonergan, Governor, about the behaviour of those who are incarcerated for this crime. I also spoke to some inmates there.

I was anxious to discover whether or not these men continued to be abusive in the confines of prison or whether they were abusive only in the safety of their own home where their victims were helpless and there was no question of retaliation.

'These men are generally well-behaved and co-operative. They are very passive and always deny the crime. They are short-term prisoners and work the system whilst inside. Often these men will be lonely and depressed in prison and have anxieties about their relationship with their partner and their desire to continue seeing their children.

'In prison they are trustworthy, model prisoners and there is no question of them being violent. Often their backgrounds are non-criminal and the shock of finding themselves in prison is enough to ensure that they do not re-offend. These prisoners are considered to be 'safe' prisoners and are not segregated within the prison. The same would not apply to those who have been jailed for sexual violence, especially against children. Sex offenders are segregated for their own protection. There is a warped sense of justice amongst prisoners regarding these offenders and they would not be safe in mainstream prison. A lot of these prisoners have themselves been battered as children.

A very low socio-economic background accounts for 95 per cent of all prisoners. Seventy-five per cent are unemployed and 40 per cent have contact with psychiatric services. No pattern has emerged for re-offending.

'I agree that the perpetrator should be removed from the family home. The wife and the children are the most important people.'

Garda Community Relations Section

The Garda Community Relations Section, based at Garda Headquarters Harcourt Square, Dublin, has issued a leaflet designed to help those who are victims of violence in the home. It is entitled 'Violence against women – help is available twenty-four hours a day'. It answers questions about the crime of rape and domestic violence and advises what one should do if one is a victim of these crimes.

Phil Power, Director, Aoibhneas Women's Refuge

'I have witnessed appalling injuries to women at the hands of men who 'love' them. Every time I think I've heard the worst imaginable horror there is always more.

'The depravity that women endure from their partners is almost unimaginable. Life for abused women can be compared to hostages trying to survive hour by hour, with no end in sight. The physical, emotional and sexual abuse of women and their children has far-reaching effects for society.

'It is estimated that one in four women in relationships experience violence in their homes. All too often, children are witness to these assaults. If we include the distressed parents, relations, friends and neighbours of women who are abused, it affects almost the entire country. We need to stop asking "*Why do women stay?*"and begin saying "*Men who assault women are criminals who are breaking the law.*"

'Family law needs to be changed to allow: barring orders for all women who need them: gardai to press charges (as in other countries) instead of the victims who are assaulted by their partners: the introduction of divorce; training for the judiciary as regards the complexities of abused women who have no visible physical evidence of abuse. Women in the refuge say over and over again how their emotional scars are far more damaging than the physical marks.

'The country was outraged when the Kilkenny Incest Case was highlighted through the media. Sadly, for all of us working in refuges, it is not an isolated case. Research has shown that the best way to protect children from being abused is to protect their mothers.

'Aoibhneas is in the process of building a much-needed refuge for the northside of Dublin. The government, Eastern Health Board and Dublin Corporation also want to see it built. The cost is £600,000. It is ironic that due to red tape in the Department of the Environment, we can only qualify for a grant of approximately half this amount. This leaves over a quarter of a million pounds to be fund-raised before the refuge can be completed.

'I urge the government to give top priority to fully funding refuges and support services and to implement changes in family law which would see that men who abuse women are held accountable by society for their actions.'

ROISIN MCDERMOTT, DIRECTOR, WOMEN'S AID
'Throughout the country there is a severe problem of overcrowding due to the lack of refuge space for women and children fleeing from violence in the home. To put this into perspective, for a population of one million, there are only sixteen refuge spaces available in the Dublin area. In this same area gardai received over thirty crisis calls per day in a four-month period.

'Women and children who are in danger of their lives and who cannot get refuge accommodation are forced into hostels for the homeless or bed and breakfast accomm-odation. This is only a temporary arrangement where women may be obliged to walk the streets with their children during the day. In the experience of Women's Aid these women are compelled to return to the violence situation due to the insecurity of this unsatisfactory arrangement. Women's Aid has been urging the govern-ment for over ten years to create a strategic plan to deal with the issue of domestic violence throughout the country. In addition to the severe shortage of refuge space, there is a frightening lack of adequate referral services for women and children. Once again we urge the government to examine the issue of domestic violence and the referral services dealing with the problem. A long-term plan is needed to protect vulnerable women and children in danger.

'We acknowledge the commitment of the Minister for Equality and Law Reform to reforming the totally inadequate Legal Aid system, and we are aware that government is committed to putting the civil Legal Aid system on a statutory basis, but would urge that this cannot wait indefinitely. Legal Aid is a civil right. It is totally unacceptable that women in abusive situations are waiting up to ten months plus for an appointment with a solicitor. Despite the fact that it is possible for women to represent themselves at district court level, it is our experience that this is not appropriate due to the trauma involved in family law cases and the ordeal of appearing before the courts.

'Violence against women violates women's human rights. It breaks bodies, families and lives. It is a grave social problem which threatens the safety, equality and bodily integrity of every woman. It must be addressed. Ultimately, it must be stopped.'

Appendix

How Not to be an Abused/Battered Woman

Don't wear make-up. If you do he'll call you a slut.

Don't not wear make-up. He'll call you a slob.

Don't ask your friends round. He won't want the house full of chattering females.

Don't not ask your friends round. Are you ashamed of him or something?

Don't have dinner on the table when he gets in. He'll think you are getting at him for being late.

Don't let dinner be late. The least a man deserves when he gets in after a long day is to have his dinner ready on the table.

Don't let the children get in his way. He'll be too tired to be bothered with a lot of screaming kids.

Don't send them to bed before he gets there. Do you want them to forget their father?

Don't ask him what kind of a day he's had. You should be able to see just by looking at him that it's been dreadful.

Don't forget to ask how his day was. A woman should show some interest in what a man's doing.

Don't tell him about your day. He doesn't want to hear a lot of complaints.

Don't not tell him about your day. Are you hiding something from him?

Don't put on a sexy negligee at bedtime. You look like a

whore, and anyway, whose money do you think you are spending?

Don't go to bed in your pyjamas. A man needs something attractive to sleep with occasionally.

Don't put your arms around him in bed. When he wants it, he'll ask for it.

Don't turn over and go to sleep. Are you frigid or what? And lastly:

Don't fight back when he hits you. It might make him worse.

Don't whatever you do, *don't* be scared. It'll make him feel guilty, so he'll hit you more.

Follow these few little tips and you'll never get battered again. Unless of course you ask for it . . .

Women's Aid, Dublin, 1993

References and Further Reading

Books

Beale, Jenny. *Women in Ireland: Voices of Change*. Dublin: Gill and Macmillan, 1986.

Brennan, Olive. *Laying Down the Law*. Dublin: Oak Tree Press, 1993.

Browne, Dervla. *Separation and Divorce Matters for Women*. Dublin: Attic Press, 1989.

Cashman, Aileen. *Money Matters for Women*. Dublin: Attic Press, 1989.

D'Orban, P. T. and A. O'Connor 'Women who kill their Parents', *British Journal of Psychiatry* 154, 27-33, 1989.

Evason, Eileen. *Hidden Violence*. Belfast: Farset Co-Op Press, 1982.

Freud, Sigmund. *New Introductory Lectures on Psychoanalysis*. Harmondsworth: Pelican, 1983.

Freud, Sigmund. *On Psychopathology*. Harmondsworth: Pelican, 1983.

Geller, Anna. *Restore your Life – Recovery from Drugs and Alcohol*. London: Thorsons, 1991.

Harris, Black, Kapla. *When Father kills Mother*. London: Routledge, 1993.

Kay, Maggie. *Children and the Law*. London: Longman, 1986.

McNeill, Keith. *How to Say No to Alcohol*. London: Sheldon Press, 1987.

O'Mahony, Paul. *Crime and Punishment in Ireland*. Dublin: Roundhall Press, 1993.

Roper, Anne. *Woman to Woman*. Dublin: Attic Press, 1986.

Russell, Diana. *Rape within Marriage*. Bloomington: Indiana University Press, 1993.

Scully D. *Understanding Sexual Violence*. Boston: Unwin Hyman, 1990.

Shanahan, Kate. *Crimes Worse than Death*. Dublin: Attic Press, 1993.

Smyth, Ailbhe. *Women's Rights in Ireland*. Dublin: Attic Press, 1983.

Smyth, Ailbhe. *Women's Rights, Children's Rights*. Dublin: Ward River Press, 1983.

Stanko, E. *Intimate Intrusions, Women's Experience of Male Violence*. London: Routledge, 1985.

Wilson, E. *What Is to be Done about Violence against Women?* Harmondsworth: Penguin, 1993.

Wilson Schaef, Anne. *When Society Becomes an Addict*. London: Thorsons, 1992.

Witherspoon, Sue. *A Woman's Place*. London: SHAC, 1985.

Wood, Kieron. *The Kilkenny Incest Case*. Dublin: Poolbeg Press, 1993.

REPORTS AND INFORMATION PACKS

Adapt House. *Abused*. Limerick, 1992.

Casey, Maeve. *Domestic Violence Against Women*. Dublin: Women's Aid, 1987.

The Council for Social Welfare. *Future Directions in Health Policy*. Dublin, 1984.

Department of Social Welfare. *Guide to Social Welfare Service*. Dublin, 1993.

Dublin Combat Poverty and Women's Aid. *Silent No More: Report on the Experience and Support Needs of Women who Have Left Abusive Relationships*. Dublin: Second Chance, 1992.

Kennedy, Anne Maria. *Working for Work*. Dublin: Irish National Organisation of the Unemployed, 1994.

Limerick Adapt Refuge and Mid-Western Health Board. *Breaking the Silence*. Policy Research Centre, 1992.

MOVE Ireland Public Information Fact Pack. MOVE: Dublin, 1991.

O'Connor, A., T. Kearney, I. Shorts, J. McCormack (Sexual Offender Programme, Central Mental Hospital). *Five-year Report April 1989 – April 1994*. Eastern Health Board, National Forensic Service, 1994.

O'Connor, M. and J. Cronin. *The Identification and Treatment of Women Admitted to an Accident and Emergency Department as a Result of Assault by Spouses/Partners*. A joint pilot project between Women's Aid and St James's Hospital. Dublin,1993.

Women's Aid Policy paper on the handling of violence against women in Ireland, 1993.

Women's Aid Submission to the Department of Equality and Law Reform on the White Paper on Marital Breakdown, 1993.

Women's Aid Submission to the Joint Oireachtas Committee on Women's Rights, 29 September1994.

Women's Aid. *Violence against Women in the Home – Why?*, 1993.

USEFUL ADDRESSES

Alcoholism, General Information
Health Promotion Unit
Hawkins House
Dublin 2
Tel: (01) 671 4711

Al-Anon (for relatives)
5 Capel Street
Dublin 1
Tel: (01) 873 2699

Alcoholics Anonymous, Service Office
109 South Circular Road
Dublin 8
Tel: (01) 453 8998 / 679 5967 (after hours)

Cherish (Association for single mothers and their rights)
2 Lower Pembroke Street
Dublin 4
Tel: (01) 668 2744

Childline
ISPCC
20 Molesworth Street
Dublin 2
Tel: 1 800 666 666 (freephone)

Drug Advisory and Treatment Centre
Trinity Court
30-31 Pearse Street
Dubin 2
Tel: (01) 677 1122

Eastern Health Board
Information and advice on health and social services
Tel: 1 800 520 520 (freephone)
(Please see local directories for other health boards and services.)

Focus Point
Emergency Accommodation Advice
14A Eustace Street
Dublin 2
Tel: (01) 671 2555

FLAC (Free Legal Advice Centres)
49 South William Street
Dublin 2
Tel: (01) 679 4239

Federation of Lone Parents
36 Upr. Rathmines Road
Dublin 6
Tel: (01) 496 4155

Gamblers Anonymous
Carmichael House
North Brunswick Street
Dublin 7
Tel: (01) 872 1133

Gingerbread (association for one-parent families)
29 Dame Street
Dublin 2
Tel: (01) 671 0291

Homeless Unit
Charles Street
Dublin 1
Tel: 1 800 724 724 (freephone)

Homeless Girls' Hostel
19 Upper Sherrard Street
Dublin 1

Legal Aid Board
Shelbourne House
Shelbourne Road
Dublin 2
Tel: 660 6011
(This board will give you details of centres in your local area.)

MOVE (Men overcoming violent experiences)
(Primarily for the abuser)
Tel: (01) 623 2540 Tuesdays 7-10 pm only.

Parentline (organisation for parents under stress)
Carmichael House
North Brunswick Street
Dublin 7
Tel: (01) 873 3500

Rape Crisis Centre
70 Lower Leeson Street
Dublin 2
Tel: (01) 661 4911/661 4564

Samaritans
Dublin 1
Tel: (01) 872 7700

Social Welfare
Information Section
Aras Mhic Dhiarmada
Store Street
Dublin 1
Tel: (01) 874 8444

Women's Aid
Carmichael House
North Brunswick Street
Dublin 7
Tel: (01) 872 3756 (Helpline)

Women's Information Network
6 Crow Street
Dublin 2
Tele: (01) 679 4700

ADDRESSES OF REFUGES

There are nine refuges in the Republic of Ireland. Staff at these refuges will give advice over the telephone. It is not necessary to visit a refuge to get advice.

Cuan Laoi (7 places)
Kyrl Street
Cork
Tel: (021) 277698

Aoibhneas (6 places)
1 Silogue Road
Ballymun
Dublin 11
Tel: (01) 842 2377

Women's Aid (10 places)
47 Lr. Rathmines Road
Dublin 6
Tel: (01) 496 1002

Waterside House (9 places)
Wood Quay
Galway
Tel: (091) 65985

Adapt House (8-10 places)
Rosbrien
Limerick
Tel: (061) 42345/42950

Women's Aid (5–8 places)
Navan
County Meath
Tel: (046) 22393

McAuley House (6 places)
Charles Street
Sligo
Tel: (071) 45682

Oasis House (9 places)
72 Morrison's Road
Waterford
Tel: (056) 70367

Bray Women's Refuge (2 places)
Bray
County Wicklow
Tel: (01) 282 9660